THE WORD MADE FLESH

Foreshadowed, Fulfilled, Forever

D1125089

Publisher: Pierre-Marie Dumont
Editor: Romain Lizé
Iconography: Isabelle Mascaras
Layout and Cover: Élise Borel
Production: Thierry Dubus, Florence Bellot, and Sabine Marioni
Proofreader: Claire Gilligan

Front cover: *The Supper at Emmaus* (detail of *Christ*, 1606), Il Caravaggio
(1573—1610), Pinacoteca di Brera, Milano, Italy. © Electa / Leemage.

Printed in July 2017 by Imprimerie Marquis, Canada
First edition: July 2017
Edition number: MGN 17027
ISBN: 978-1-941709-49-8

FR. RICHARD VERAS

THE WORD MADE FLESH

Foreshadowed, Fulfilled, Forever

MAGNIFICAT

Paris • New York • Oxford • Madrid

TABLE OF CONTENTS

FOREWORD

Once, during a high school religion class, an exasperated student said to me, "Father, you talk about Jesus as if he's here." I was moved that he noticed that we spoke of Jesus in our Scripture class in a different way than Washington or Lincoln was spoken about in his history class. Jesus is most certainly historical (*The Word became flesh and dwelt among us*); but the Church claims just as certainly that he is living and present (Msgr. Luigi Giussani prayed that phrase of the Angelus as "The Word became flesh and *dwells* among us.")

The student's exasperation was understandable. If Jesus dwells among us, then where is he? And that was the student's next question. When I told him that Jesus is with us, he didn't let me off the hook, but insisted "Where is he? Which desk is he sitting in?" This question was neither disrespectful nor ironic; it was reasonable. I did not receive it as an objection to what I was teaching, but as a sincere inquiry from a student who was seriously engaged.

I explained that when students in the class asked questions or offered unexpected comments that brought us more deeply into the Scriptures and mysteries we were studying, this was Jesus manifesting himself through them to correct and guide me. At this point another student demanded, "When? Name names." I proceeded to offer instances when this occurred and to name the students who at those moments were, for me, the presence of Christ. The students became eager to hear their names mentioned; for the claim that can God can be that closely and concretely present to us is ever new. This is, in fact, is the promise of Jesus, Emmanuel, God with us.

Jesus promises to be *with us always* (cf. Mt 28:20), and who is Jesus? He is the Word made flesh, the Incarnation, the enfleshment of the divine, God who became present in a human face. At the Last Supper, when Philip demanded of Jesus, *Master, show us the Father,* Jesus responded, *Have I been with you for so long a time and you still do not know me, Philip? Whoever has seen me has seen the Father* (Jn 14:8-9).

Philip was the precursor of the student in my class that day. He asked essentially the same question, "Where is God?" and Jesus' answer to Philip is that God has been and still is present to him through the very face of Jesus. And if this same Jesus promises to be with us always, his presence among us must involve faces and come to us through the flesh, not only in the time of the Apostles, but now.

In another class a student told me of his seemingly miraculous survival of a car accident that he was in as a child. He asked me if this was an experience of Jesus. I responded that it was certainly an experience of God, but I don't know that it was an experience of Jesus. He and the other students became very upset with me. I explained that I would like each of them to have a continual and stable way of responding to and relating to God, but that surviving near death experiences would be a spectacularly inconvenient method by which to do that. What characterizes Jesus is that he is in a place, he has a face. I can seek him out, I can return to him. I can go back to that youth group, to that parish, to that sacrament, to that family, to that priest, to that friend. That student cannot return to that car accident; and if he does not find God in the flesh here and now in his present and as a promise for his future, then that accident does not become a point of change and conversion, but a curious and moving incident to bring up in religion class or when dinner conversation might take a spiritual turn.

Saint Bernard once preached, "Before the Son of God became man his goodness was hidden, for God's mercy is eternal, but how could such goodness be recognized? It was promised, but it was not experienced, and as a result few believed in it."[1]

I was raised Catholic, and received witness from my parents and family. I was brought to the sacraments, and I received further witness and catechesis from teachers and priests. Thus, Christ was forming me and calling me through the flesh of my family, through the faces of those he placed in my path in the parish, the school, and the religious education program. But, like Philip, I had been with Jesus for a long time and did not know him. I thought of him as somewhere in the heavens, loving me, but from afar. I admired him greatly and worshipped him, sometimes formalistically and sometimes sincerely. And I believe I loved him, too, but from afar.

As a young college graduate living and working in Manhattan, I was certainly seeking him. And one day a priest recommended to me a group of young workers who met at Saint Patrick's Cathedral. In March of 1988 I went to my first meeting. These were my peers; they were like me. However, there was a joy among them that was evident that first day. As time went on, I discovered that these young men and women had become friends and saw each other outside of the weekly meeting. They were sharing life together. As I remained and entered into this friendship, I noticed that it was a friendship different than what I had experienced in high school or college or among co-workers. It somehow reached to the core of who I am. The experience was that of being welcomed as you were, and at the same time being invited to something truer. There was a sense of belonging that went deeper than our ability to be kind to one another or to agree with each other. It is difficult to describe, which is why the earliest Christian proposal was to "come and see." This is what Jesus proposed to John and Andrew, and what they proposed to Peter, and what Philip would propose to Nathaniel (Jn 1:35ff).

The group to which I was referred is Communion and Liberation, a lay movement that arose from the faith, missionary zeal, and genius of the Servant of God Monsignor Luigi Giussani. Msgr. Giussani was an expert educator who tirelessly pointed to the fact that the exceptionality of Christ was something noticeable to any human being, even if you were not religious or "spiritual"; and that this exceptionality continues among the members of his Church, which is the continuation of his presence in history. It is an exceptionality that cannot always be explained, but whose existence is palpable, real, in the flesh, something that can be pointed to, returned to, experienced, lived with.

Giussani reminded his original high school students that Jesus said, *where two or three are gathered in my name, there am I in the midst of them* (Mt 18:20). He proposed that they meet outside of class time and share life together, whether playing games, or discussing art or politics or science, or seeing movies, or going on vacations or retreats. He told them to do this keeping Christ in mind, and to verify whether they see something different in the way they are friends and in the way they approach reality around them. If they experience something different, then they must take seriously the possibility that the difference is Christ present in their midst.

That proposal reached me through those young workers at Saint Patrick's Cathedral, and that initial and impressive encounter did not become a nostalgic memory for me, but a way to experience and eventually to recognize the presence of Christ in his Church. It is as if Jesus spoke to me as he spoke to Philip and said, "If you have seen the exceptionality of this friendship, the love and belonging of these people who are flawed sinners like you, then you have seen me present in their midst, and through me you have seen the face of the Father.... I am with you." Saint Paul speaks of this real presence of Jesus in the midst of his Church as a *treasure in earthen vessels* (2 Cor 4:7).

Jesus began to be an experience in my life through Communion and Liberation. It has happened for others through another movement in the Church, or a vibrant parish, or an active youth group, or a faithful campus ministry, or an alive religious community, or a family. Growing up my parents had a number of friends who were not of our faith and lived life very differently from us, but who loved to visit our family and be around us. Was it possibly Jesus in our midst that so attracted them?

As time went by my involvement in Communion and Liberation led me to love Jesus more and more, or rather, to respond more and more to his love for me, which was continually verified as I followed this particular place in his Church. I discerned a call to the priesthood through Jesus' presence in our midst. Through the ensuing years, when students have asked me why I became a priest, I tell them it is for the same reason that a man falls in love with a woman and asks her to marry him. I met Jesus and fell in love. It is that simple and that mysterious; it is the Incarnation.

When I began my seminary studies, especially my Scripture classes, I wondered if my youthful enthusiasm would be tempered and I would be shown that Jesus, the Word made flesh, is not really quite so close to us. Perhaps I would have to "grow up" and see that I had overdone it a little, or perhaps Msgr. Giussani had exaggerated a bit.

What I share with you in this book is that the Good News is *really that good*; God is really with us in ways we can see and touch and dwell with. In class after class that I took in the seminary, and in preparing for class after class that I have taught throughout my priesthood, I see that, over and over, Scripture promises and witnesses to us the Good News of Jesus Christ, the Word made flesh, who dwells among us.

Introduction

❦

It Was Not a Messenger or an Angel, but He Himself Who Saved Them   (Is 63:9)

Now there were shepherds in that region living in the fields and keeping the night watch over their flock. The angel of the Lord appeared to them and the glory of the Lord shone around them, and they were struck with great fear. The angel said to them, "Do not be afraid; for behold, I proclaim to you good news of great joy that will be for all the people. For today in the city of David a savior has been born for you who is Messiah and Lord. And this will be a sign for you: you will find an infant wrapped in swaddling clothes and lying in a manger." And suddenly there was a multitude of the heavenly host with the angel, praising God and saying:

"Glory to God in the highest / and on earth peace to those on whom his favor rests."

When the angels went away from them to heaven, the shepherds said to one another, "Let us go, then, to Bethlehem to see this thing that has taken place, which the Lord has made known to us." So they went in haste and found Mary and Joseph, and the infant lying in the manger. When they saw this, they made known the message that had been told them about this child. All who heard it were amazed by what had been told them by the shepherds. And Mary kept all these things, reflecting on them in her heart. (Lk 2:8-19)

What No Angel Could Do

In his book *The Angels and Their Mission According to the Fathers of the Church*, Cardinal Jean Daniélou has a chapter about the angels rejoicing at the Birth of Christ. He cites Fathers of the Church to explain why the multitude of angels was praising God so joyously. Saint John Chrysostom, Origen, and Eusebius all preached and wrote about the general lack of success the angels were having in bringing men and women to God. The angels were obeying God and looking after his creation; but human beings, having been given free will, are very different from the rest of God's visible creation, and the angels saw that it was difficult, perhaps impossible, for spirits like themselves to move the hearts of flesh and blood men and women.

In the Gospel of Luke, each time an angel is sent to speak to a person, the angel at some point says, *Do not be afraid* (see Lk 1:13, 1:30, 2:10). We humans are earthly, not just spirit but flesh; and so a disembodied spirit is way outside of our comfort zone and thus unlikely to attract at first sight.

For instance, I am not a big fan of the dark; and in one of the parishes where I served, the lights for the gym were on the opposite end from the exit door, a full basketball court away. Often enough I would be the last one in there after an evening event and would have to turn off the lights. I admit that after turning them off I would usually walk briskly to the exit. Now, during that brisk walk, should an angel have appeared and tried to reassure me, I can assure you that it would have had the opposite of the desired effect.

What doesn't scare me? Babies do not scare me. Neither do children or adults. In fact, if another person was with me when I turned out those lights, the dark was not scary at all, and I could walk peacefully.

Now consider that God, like the angels, is also Spirit. And although we are made in his image, as Genesis tells us, our response to him is often one of fear.

With this in mind, the angels' rejoicing makes a lot of sense. Since we are made in the image of God, our hearts at their core are longing for him; however, pure spirit is strange to us and instills fear. So angels will not have much success with us. Human prophets will also have limited success, because they are fallen human beings like us. What do we need? We need God to come and attract us to himself. Isaiah expressed this when he said, *Oh that you would rend the heavens and come down* (Is 63:19). But God as God can scare us much more than any angel. We will see in a later chapter how God's own chosen people backed away from him when he tried to reveal himself to them at Horeb (Dt 18:16, see pp. 58-60). So how can God approach us without our backing away? How can he invite us into a relationship with him? By taking flesh and dwelling among us, i.e., by mysteriously bringing the fullness of his divinity to dwell in a man of flesh and blood.

The angels rejoice that God has come to the rescue of mankind by becoming a man, and their mission from this moment on will be to point men and women to Jesus, the man through whom God is with us, the man through whom God can save us. The shepherds may have been afraid of an angel, but they were not afraid of the baby to whom the angels pointed.

What the Shepherds Saw

Why do the angels tell the shepherds not to be afraid? Because a child has been born. God who comes in the flesh can allay our fear. He can live among us and attract us to himself by sharing in our humanity.

Shepherds were just about the most humble, most earthy people to whom the angels could have been sent to make their heavenly proclamation. In the time of Jesus, the occupation of the shepherd placed one under suspicion of theft and sinfulness, similar to that of the publican.[2] And so the very first proclamation of his coming into the world, after those made to his family, is made to shepherds. The image of the heavenly angels and the earthly shepherds rejoicing together is itself an iconic harbinger of the Incarnation, the heavenly in communion with the earthly.

This humble group of shepherds will be the first guests of the Holy Family. Uneducated men, unfavored by the respectably religious people of their time and place, are the first after Mary and Joseph to gaze upon the Word made flesh, who had only just begun to make his dwelling among us.

There is an Italian song, *I Pastori,* sung from the point of view of one of the shepherds, which is beautifully expressive of the mystery of the Incarnation. The shepherd recalls that it was a day and night like any other, he and his companions shepherding their sheep and sleeping in the fields, when the angels broke into the night with an awakening voice and a splendid light, "and the angel said to go and to take the short road to Bethlehem, and we found the stable, and the child crying in the cold…and he was God."

Mary and Joseph

Jesus, the Son of God, did not merely *appear* to be human, he really *became* human. In the Old Testament there are times when God appears as if in human form, such as when he walks in the garden looking for Adam and Eve (Gn 3:8), or when he wrestles with Jacob at the ford of the Jabbok (Gn 32:23-31, see p. 44-47). While these moments are foreshadowings of the Incarnation, appearing human and becoming human are not the same thing. Humans don't just appear; we are born of a woman, we grow into adulthood through time and in particular places, and we die.

That Jesus is born of Mary assures us that he has really become human. A Catholic friend of mine was once permitted by her Evangelical daughter to bring her four-year-old granddaughter to the Catholic church one Sunday morning. As they were leaving Mass, the young girl saw a statue on the front lawn of the church. In the church where she normally went, this girl heard a lot about Jesus from people who love him, but she had not yet heard about Mary. When she asked her grandmother about the statue, and was told that it was a statue of Mary, the Mother of Jesus, her response was, "Jesus had a mother??!!" What caused such awe? The Incarnation. That little girl had discovered that Jesus has a Mother, like us. He really became flesh. He did not just appear human, he became human.

Luke's Gospel tells us that, like every other human, Jesus grew *in wisdom and age* (Lk 2:52). Human beings learn and grow over time, and we learn from our parents. How could Jesus, who is God, learn from Mary and Joseph, who are lowly humans? Because Jesus is God who has become truly human. Recall that Gabriel responded to Mary, who asked, *How can this be?* (Lk 1:34) by assuring her that *nothing will be impossible for God* (Lk 1:37).

The visit of the shepherds gives us a hint into the way Mary faced reality. Having given birth to Jesus in this most inconvenient place, what could be less welcome than a group of strangers entering your humble abode? Strangers who not only smelled of their sheep but were suspected by many to be sinners. However, Mary does not object. She does not recoil but instead ponders with awe what God has begun to do in their midst. What is the meaning of these shepherds being invited so close to God?

Is it from Mary that Jesus would learn to welcome tax collectors and public sinners, lepers and the blind? Does Jesus resemble his Mother when he refuses to send the hungry crowds away when the Apostles ask him to do so (Mk 6:36)? When Jesus is in the garden accepting to suffer and die, does he resemble his Mother, who accepted the prophecy of Simeon that her Son would be *contradicted and that she herself would be pierced by a sword* (cf. Lk 2:34-35)?

And let us not forget Joseph. If you visit Bethlehem there is a Grotto of Saint Joseph close to the place of Jesus' Birth. Surely those shepherds could not have gazed upon Jesus and Mary without the permission of the husband, father, and protector of the Holy Family. Joseph's presence in the life of the boy Jesus also confirms the true humanity of the Son of God. A human child needs to receive fatherly love from a flesh and blood man, whether that man be a biological or adoptive father or an uncle or a grandfather or another family friend. Jesus needed to look at and learn from Saint Joseph how to be a man, how to be a father. The human development of Jesus required the presence of Joseph.

In times past, God spoke in partial and various ways to our ancestors through the prophets; in these last days, he spoke to us through a son…/ who is the refulgence of his glory,/ the very imprint of his being. (Heb 1:1-3)

Humans don't just appear. We have ancestors, we have a history. Let us look at the history which not only led to but mysteriously foreshadowed the event of the Incarnation.

PART I

<small>THE FORESHADOWING
OF CHRIST</small>

CHAPTER 1

❦

Genesis of Creation, Promise of Salvation, Foreshadowing of the Incarnation

The Protoevangelium

The Church teaches us that God promised Jesus to us at the very outset of human existence, right after the Fall of our first parents.

How does God respond to the original sin? With his perceptible presence. As stated in the previous chapter, God had not yet become human, but his presence in the garden is through a seemingly ordinary human form (Gn 3:8). That Adam and Eve are familiar with God's presence in their dwelling is evidenced when they recognize the sounds in the garden to be him.

God's concern for them is expressed in his first words to them after the fall, *Where are you?* (Gn 3:9). It is important to note that the fear that drove our first parents into hiding was not rooted in God's presence itself, for it seems they have been comfortable with his presence up to this point; their fear stems from their shame at their sin and their nakedness. It is they who distance themselves from God; it is not God who recoils from them. They want to hide, but God asks them, *Where are you?*

After discerning from their demeanor what has happened, God speaks to the serpent, the woman, and the man of the sad consequences of Original Sin. Yet in the midst of this dark litany, the Church assures us that there is a spark of light. In Genesis 3:15 God says to the serpent, *I will put enmity between you and the woman,/ and between your offspring and hers;/ He will strike at your head,/ while you strike at his heel.* The Church calls this the Protoevangelium, the "First Gospel." Fathers of the Church propose that the *woman* is Mary, the "New Eve" who will obediently become the Mother of Jesus, who himself is the "New Adam" whose obedient Death on the cross will strike the head of the serpent. By undoing Adam's disobedience Jesus will win victory over the evil rooted in sin. In the Exsultet at the Easter

Vigil the Church sings that the promised light is greater than all the darkness of sin: "O truly necessary sin of Adam, destroyed completely by the Death of Christ! O happy fault that earned so great, so glorious a Redeemer!"[3]

In John's Gospel Jesus himself is likely referring to God's promise in Genesis 3:15 when he uncharacteristically refers to his Mother as *woman* at two pivotal moments in his battle against the evil brought about by the serpent: at the beginning of his public ministry, at the wedding feast of Cana—*Woman, how does your concern affect me?* (Jn 2:4)—and at the culmination of his public ministry, when from his victorious cross he says *Woman, behold, your son* (Jn 19:26). After the fall, the first Adam calls his wife Eve, *because she became the mother of all the living* (Gn 3:20). From the cross the New Adam calls his Mother *woman*, and she becomes the Mother of all the redeemed.

In considering the young girl I wrote about, who was moved to discover that Jesus had a Mother, it is interesting that the Protoevangelium mentions the woman first, and then her offspring. It is thus clear that the Redeemer will be human, born from a mother. It is yet hidden in the Heart of God that the Redeemer will be God himself, not merely appearing in the form of a human, but truly becoming human and dwelling among us.

Pre-Protoevangelium: The Creation Accounts

Let's look even further back than the Proto-evangelium. Before the God's word proclaims the First Gospel in Genesis 3:15, God hinted at the promised Incarnation in the very creation accounts that begin the Book of Genesis.

Before proceeding, it is important to note that these accounts are not claiming to be scientific expositions. They deal with something much more profound than science. Why, for instance, are there chaplains in hospitals? Why are there bereavement groups? A physician can usually explain the disease behind our symptoms. A medical examiner investigates and explains the reason for physical death. But our questions before suffering and death are more profound than science can explain. In these situations, the question of "Why?" is not answered by a merely physical, scientific explanation. That "Why?" is at the level of "Why is this happening to me?" "Why do suffering and death exist at all?" "What is the meaning behind this?" It is at the level of these questions that we approach the creation accounts in Genesis; for they delve into the primordial questions: "Who is God?" "Who am I?"

The Bible begins with two creation stories, whose literary origins scholars trace to different moments in the chosen people's history. The differing circumstances give rise to divergent viewpoints. The second creation account, the older of the two, is thought to have been written when the chosen people were thriving in their own land, indeed their own kingdom, and it describes particular people and a particular land. The first account is thought to have been written after the fall of the northern and southern kingdoms, when the chosen people were exiled from their land; this may be why it is written from a more universal, perhaps spiritual perspective. Note that the formation of the Bible itself is in harmony with the Incarnation. God used the humanity and the particular circumstances of the sacred writers in order to communicate divine truth. While the two creation accounts have distinct origins and emphases, they contain an inspired complementarity.

In the first account, God just says things and they happen. *God said, "Let there be light," and there was light…. "Let there be a dome…." And so it happened* (Gn 1:3, 6). This God is beyond his creation, exercising a power beyond human experience. He is a God who is not present within the world he is creating, but far above it. Even when he ultimately speaks to the men and women he creates in his image, you have a sense of a disembodied voice commanding from afar. This God certainly seems divine.

In the second creation story, God is within the world he has created. He does not omnipotently utter commands; he has to work to create, just like we have to. He molds man out of the clay of the ground; he blows into his nostrils. He plants a garden. He forms animals out of the ground. He takes one of Adam's ribs from him and builds a woman. He will make clothes for Adam and Eve. He seems to have a physical body: hands to work, lungs to breathe, just like us. He will walk in the garden and his movements will make noise, just like ours do. He is not a voice communicating from afar; he speaks with Adam and Eve face to face, because he dwells within creation. This God seems human.

The first account: God who is beyond, above, divine. The second account: God who works and walks and dwells in the world, like a human. The chosen people pride themselves on their monotheism, for they have been chosen to receive the revelation that there is one God. So their two different accounts are meant to portray one and the same God. And what do they tell us? That God is far above us and yet comes close to us. He is both beyond his creation and within his creation. He is infinitely incomprehensible and yet familiar. Thus the first creation accounts, the very genesis of Genesis, seem to prophesy Jesus, the Son of God who will be fully divine and fully human.

Let us now consider what these accounts say about us. The first account tells us that God has made us in his image. This would explain our limitless aspirations and our insatiable longing for love. God is Infinite Being and we are infinite need. The second account tells us that we are made of clay. This explains our weakness. Our lives are fleeting, heading toward dust. And even during our lives we often find that *we don't do the good we want to do and we engage in the evil we don't want to do* (cf. Rom 7:19). Who can save such strange beings who have an undying urge for divinity housed in mortal fragility? Saint Paul answers, *Jesus Christ* (Rom 7:25).

Our human existence itself is a cry for and a prophecy of Jesus. For he alone can bring peace to our spiritual and carnal condition when he communicates his divinity to us in the only way we can receive it, through his humanity. Thus God does not only promise Jesus through the written words of Scripture; he has inscribed this promise at the very core of our mysterious human existence.

For you my body yearns;
for you my soul thirsts. (Ps 63:2)

My soul yearns and pines
for the courts of the LORD.
My heart and flesh cry out
for the living God. (Ps 84:3)

All flesh shall see the salvation of God. (Lk 3:6)

What was from the beginning
what we have heard,
what we have seen with our eyes,
what we looked upon
and touched with our hands
concerns the Word of life—
for the life was made visible:
we have seen it and testify to it
and proclaim to you the eternal life
that was with the Father and was made
     visible to us.
     (1 Jn:1-2)

Chapter 2

❧❧❧

Abraham, Isaac, and Jacob…and Esau

Abraham and Sarah…and Isaac

While the creation stories seek to explain the origin of all humanity as made by God, the story of Abraham recounts God's choice of one specific man, whom he calls by name. And through this one man God chooses a particular people. God's preference for the particular sets into motion the history of salvation, which will culminate in the Incarnation of his Only Begotten Son, a particular man who will live in a particular place and time.

Abraham is old and his wife Sarah is beyond childbearing years. Yet God promises to Abraham that he will have a son born of Sarah, and through this heir Abraham will have descendants as numerous as the stars in the sky. Abraham finds this promise to be somewhat preposterous, and even laughs at it (Gn 17:17). He tries to temper God's promise and recommends that Ishmael, the son he had with Sarah's servant Hagar, would be just fine with him. God pays no attention to this and responds, *Nevertheless, your wife Sarah is to bear you a son, and you shall call him Isaac* (Gn 17:19).

When this promise reaches Sarah's ears, she, too, will find it laughable. God questions Sarah's laugh and affirms that nothing is too marvelous for him to do (words later echoed by Gabriel to Mary). Sarah claims she didn't laugh, and God responds to her lie with a simple and direct, *Yes you did* (Gn 18:15). No further correction or punishment was necessary; this likely pierced Sarah to the core.

Once, when teaching a confirmation class in a parish, a student was quite flippant as she casually lied about her missing assignment. This was not behavior I had never seen in a student before, yet for some reason I was moved to ask her simply and directly, "Are you lying to me?" The reason I remember asking the question is because of her response. Her demeanor immediately changed and she looked at me with an expression somewhere between distress and sadness. She had no words to respond, and I did not pursue the matter further. The following week she approached me with a sincere and moving apology, and her presence in class was different from that day forward. A few years later I was invited back to my old parish to give a talk…and there she was, now a high school student, who came to the talk and brought her mother, and made it a point to greet me afterward and thank me for that class. That correction had pierced her more deeply than I had ever intended…but God seems to have known what he was doing.

Sarah, after laughing at God and lying to him, may have been tempted to temper her own hope in his promise. However, in Genesis 21:1, we have one of the most momentous verses in all of Hebrew Scripture, *The LORD took note of Sarah as he had said he would; he did for her as he had promised.* God revealed himself to be faithful and merciful; and his mercy was made known through the coming of a beloved son.

Sarah rejoices and proclaims, *God has given me cause to laugh, and all who hear of it will laugh with me* (Gn 21:6). The discovery that God is faithful to his promise even when we do not trust him is the reason for this pure and joyful laughter of Sarah, and of all who will come to know this event and laugh with her. In fact, the name Isaac is a form of the Hebrew word for laughter.

For Abraham and Sarah, God's mercy is not an abstract or spiritual truth that they have learned; it has taken flesh in their son Isaac. Any time they might again be tempted to doubt or temper God's promise of mercy, they need only look at their son. That his name means laughter will remind them of their doubt, not in order to discourage them, but to increase their rejoicing in the love that meets sin with mercy—visible, tangible mercy. Isaac is an incarnation of God's love for Abraham and Sarah, and for us he is a foreshadowing of the Incarnation of God's Only Begotten Son.

Isaac will be all the more a type of Jesus when God asks Abraham to sacrifice his beloved son. Isaac will follow his father up the mountain carrying wood on his shoulders. He will question his father, asking about the sheep for the sacrifice. Abraham will tell Isaac that God himself will provide the lamb. Isaac will submit when his father ties him up. And he will be saved from death by God's intervention (Gn 22:1-19).

Jesus will question his Father as to whether he must be the lamb that God provides. He will carry the wood of the cross on his shoulders. He will submit to being lifted high on the cross, because he will trust his Father's promise. And we will be saved from death by God's beloved Son.

If he give his life as an offering for sin,
he shall see his descendants in a long life. (Is 53:10)

Like water my life drains away....
So wasted are my hands and feet
that I can count all my bones....
They divide my garments among them;
for my clothing they cast lots.
But you, LORD, do not stay far off;
my strength, come quickly to help me....
For God has not spurned or disdained
the misery of this poor wretch,

Did not turn away from me,
but heard me when I cried out....
I will live for the LORD;
my descendants will serve you.
  (Ps 22:15, 17b-18a, 19-20, 25, 31)

Jacob and Esau

Isaac will grow up to marry Rebekah, who will also be sterile until Isaac entreats the Lord and the Lord answers his prayer twofold. Rebekah becomes pregnant with twins who already struggle with one another in her womb. The first to be born is Esau, followed by his brother Jacob. Isaac preferred Esau, the skillful hunter who lived out in the open, and Rebekah preferred Jacob, who stayed close to home (Gn 24–25).

Jacob was clever, and he bargained his older brother out of his birthright in exchange for lentil stew that he had made (Esau was really hungry).

Later, as Isaac comes to the end of his life, he asks Esau to hunt and prepare a meal for him, promising that after he eats it he will give Esau a special blessing before he dies. After Esau obediently goes out to hunt, Rebekah conspires with Jacob to deceive Isaac and receive for himself the blessing that was promised to Esau. Jacob gets the goats and Rebekah prepares the meal. She then puts some of Esau's clothes on Jacob as well as goatskins on his arms and neck, so that he will smell and feel like Esau when he approaches Isaac, whose eyesight has failed him in his old age. The scheme works, and Jacob receives Isaac's blessing.

When Esau brings to his father the meal he has prepared from the game he hunted, they both come realize that Jacob had duped Isaac and received his blessing. Isaac explains that the blessing is irrevocable, and Esau sobs loudly and bitterly that his brother Jacob has not only taken his birthright, but has now tricked him out of his father's blessing. Esau is so distraught that he plans to kill Jacob after the period of mourning for Isaac has passed.

Rebekah, fearing for Jacob's life, sends him to her brother Laban in Haran, telling Jacob to stay there until Esau's anger subsides (Gn 27:1-45).

Jacob goes to Haran and falls in love with Laban's daughter Rachel, and he promises to serve Laban for seven years to win Rachel's hand in marriage. At the end of the seven years Laban tricks Jacob into consummating a marriage instead with his older daughter Leah (what goes around comes around). Laban gives Rachel to Jacob a week later in exchange for another seven years of service. During his time with Laban, Jacob begets eleven sons and a daughter with Leah, Rachel, and their respective maidservants Zilpah and Bilhah. (The twelfth son, Benjamin, will come after Jacob returns to his homeland.) Jacob also came to own large flocks, camels, and asses, as well as male and female servants. (Some trickery was involved in gaining the flocks, which you can read about in Gn 30:25ff).

In Genesis 31:3 the Lord says to Jacob, *Return to the land of your fathers…and I will be with you*. Although it is at least fourteen years later, Jacob is still concerned about Esau's anger, and sends messengers before him in the hope of gaining his favor. When the messengers return to tell Jacob that Esau is coming to meet him accompanied by four hundred men, Scripture tells us that *Jacob was very much frightened* (Gn 32:8). Clever as always, Jacob divides his belongings and servants into two camps so that, if Esau attacks one, he will at least be left with the other.

Then he prays to God, *O God of my father Abraham and God of my father Isaac! You told me, O LORD, "Go back to the land of your birth, and I will be good to you."… Save me, I pray, from the hand of my brother Esau* (Gn 32:10, 12). Leaving nothing to chance, Jacob then sets aside hundreds from among his livestock to send forth to Esau, for he reasons, *If I first appease him with gifts that precede me, then later, when I face him, perhaps he will forgive me* (Gn 32:21). With this appeasement offering, Jacob is shrewdly trying to negotiate forgiveness.

An Unexpected Encounter

Just as we are building up to the showdown, scripture abruptly turns our attention to another scene. During the night, Jacob has to help his wives and children to cross the ford of the Jabbok. After doing this he is left alone, until out of nowhere someone emerges and wrestles with him until dawn. Let us welcome this strange interruption, because we will soon find out that it is actually an important prelude.

Jacob's wrestling opponent is described as some man. After a long struggle the man strikes Jacob's hip and tells Jacob to let him go. But Jacob will not let his mysterious opponent go until the man blesses him. Jacob has thus concluded that this man is holy. At this point the man changes Jacob's name to Israel, because, he says, *You have contended with divine and human beings and have prevailed* (Gn 32:29). When Jacob asks the man his name, the man does not tell him but bids him farewell. Note that God is the one who changes names in Scripture, and God himself is unnameable because his mystery is too great to be expressed in a name. Thus Jacob proclaims, *I have seen God face to face* (Gn 32:31).

In this unexpected encounter Jacob foreshadowed the path that every Christian will have to travel. First some man enters his life. This is not a mere spiritual entrance, but quite physical. In fact, it is physical enough to leave Jacob with a limp. As the struggle ensues, Jacob concludes that there is something holy about this man, and as he continues to pay attention to what this man does and says, he concludes that this man is God. As we noted earlier (p. 21), God is here merely appearing in human form; he has not become human. However, he is certainly laying down a blueprint for what will happen in the encounter with Jesus.

Jesus looked to be like any other man. His demeanor was so ordinary that John the Baptist had to point him out. Very quickly those who follow him begin to realize that there is something exceptional, something holy about him. As time goes on, those who consider seriously what he says and does may come to believe that he is God. We follow the same path with the person or the community of people through whom we have encountered Jesus. After being attracted by their exceptionality, if we welcome them into our lives and take note of why they are the way they are, we come to recognize Christ in the midst of them, and believe in him.

A woman I met during a parish mission told me that she had become Catholic because she experienced a joy in her fiancé's family that was fascinating and attractive to her, and as time passed she came to the conclusion that the source of their evident joy was their faith in Jesus. This recognition, over time, led to her faith in Jesus.

Jacob emerged with a limp. The life of every Christian, like the life of that young woman, is indelibly marked by the encounter with Christ.

Another Encounter, Just as Unexpected

From the struggle with God we return to the struggle with Esau. After Jacob emerges from his struggle and marvels, *I have seen God face to face*, he looks up and sees Esau coming. Still quite concerned, he arranges his wives and maidservants and children, the least preferred in the front (first to go down in case of an attack) and most preferred in the back. Jacob goes before them and bows to the ground seven times.

And then, once again, out of nowhere, something happens.

Esau ran to meet him, embraced him, and flinging himself on his neck, kissed him as he wept (Gn 33:4).

Esau weeps for joy to see his brother again. He looks up in gleeful amazement at Jacob's family. He is clearly happy that his brother has prospered.

Then Esau asked, "What did you intend with all those droves that I encountered?"

Jacob answered, "It was to gain my lord's favor" (Gn 33:8).

Esau, at this point, is truly a man with no guile. He is overjoyed to see his brother. Whatever grudge he bore after Jacob's deception is so far gone, so long healed, that he cannot even imagine why Jacob would send him gifts. Jacob has shrewdly prepared for this meeting; but Esau needs no such preparation; he loves his brother. He is not interested in his brother's gifts; it is his younger brother himself who moves him to this magnanimous welcome.

"I have plenty," replied Esau; "you should keep what is yours, brother."

"No, I beg you!" said Jacob. "If you will do me the favor, please accept this gift from me, since to

come into your presence is for me like coming into the presence of God, now that you have received me so kindly" (Gn 33:9-10).

This encounter is just as unexpected as the one Jacob had with God himself at the ford of the Jabbok. In a very real sense, this is a second encounter with God. When Jacob tells Esau that to come into his presence is to come into the presence of God, he is not speaking figuratively. These words are spoken by a man who has just seen God face to face. If the first encounter left Jacob with a limp, this encounter is perhaps even more impactful. It brings about in Jacob an inward conversion. As at the Jabbok Jacob prefigured the path of the Christian, here Jacob prefigures what redemption can look like. Jacob is so moved by Esau's love that the gifts that were originally planned as an appeasement become a pure offering. Jacob begs Esau to take his gifts. He has moved from calculation to love. He could not have produced this movement in himself; he was moved by Esau.

Recall also what God promised Jacob when he told him to embark on this journey, *Return to the land of your fathers...and I will be with you* (Gn 31:3). Jacob never could have imagined that God would be with him through the face of his brother Esau. Quite the contrary, Jacob had prayed that God would save him from Esau. Just as God did not pay attention when Abraham offered to settle for Ishmael rather than have a son with Sarah (Gn 17:18), God did not pay attention to Jacob's request.

Being with Jacob at the Jabbok was not enough. God was promising Jacob so much more. And so God comes to Jacob in Esau. And how did Jacob recognize God's presence in his brother? *You have received me so kindly* (Gn 33:10). For Jacob, God's mercy has taken flesh. And nowhere could it have been revealed more powerfully than through the brother that Jacob had deceived. The brother whom he so feared because he had sinned against him so grievously. O happy fault! O truly necessary sin of Jacob!

How could we say that God did something greater through Esau then he did with his more immediate presence at the Jabbok? We can look to the woman who proclaimed, *My soul pro-*

claims the greatness of the Lord (Lk 1:46). When God took flesh and became a Baby in her womb, his love was more greatly magnified for Mary and for the chosen people than it had ever been before. Could anything more expressively reveal his love for us and his desire to be with us than taking upon himself our frail flesh? And even that would not be enough; he would go to the cross and take upon himself our sins.

Jacob wondered at the mystery of seeing God face to face at the Jabbok, but when he saw God in the face of Esau, when he felt the embrace of the brother whom he had deceived, and saw the purity of his brother's love, Jacob's awe was magnified immeasurably. In the flesh of Esau he discovered the infinity of God's mercy, as his grandmother Sarah had discovered the mystery of his mercy in the flesh of her son Isaac, and as his descendant Mary would discover the fulfillment of God's mercy in the Babe in her womb, her Son Jesus.

Infinite divinity manifested and magnified in the finite frailty of a human face? *Nothing will be impossible for God.*

My soul proclaims the greatness of the Lord.
My spirit rejoices in God my savior.
For he has looked with favor on his lowly servant....
He has mercy on those who fear him
in every generation....
He has come to the help of his servant Israel,
for he has remembered his promise of mercy,
the promise he made to our fathers,
to Abraham and his children forever.

    (Lk 1:46-48a, 50, 54-55)

Chapter 3

Moses and the Prophet, David and the King

God's Presence through Human Frailty

Moses is one of the most significant figures through whom the Hebrew Scriptures reveal that God becomes mysteriously and truly present through frail human flesh.

To escape Pharaoh's death sentence for newborn Hebrew boys, Moses' family placed him in a basket in the river, where he was discovered and adopted by Pharaoh's daughter. As a young man, Moses fled Pharaoh's house after it became known that he killed an Egyptian for striking a Hebrew, whom Moses knew was his true kin.

Long after he left Egypt, on a day when he was tending the flock of his father-in-law, Moses saw a bush that was burning but was not consumed by the fire. He approached to look more closely. From this exceptional sight, the voice of God called Moses to lead the Israelites out of slavery in Egypt to freedom.

Moses objected, *Who am I that I should go to Pharaoh and lead the Israelites out of Egypt?* and God responded, *I will be with you* (Ex 3:11-12). But Moses needed reassurance to help him trust God, and so God revealed to Moses a name by which he could be designated (*I AM*), and showed him signs of his authority.

But Moses still objected, *If you please, LORD, I have never been eloquent, neither in the past, nor recently, nor now that you have spoken to your servant; but I am slow of speech and tongue* (Ex 4:10).

Since he is being called to bear God's authority to Pharaoh, Moses expects that God should take this conspicuous weakness away from him. In fact, Moses seems to think that God should already have taken it away, for he notes that he still has this speech impediment even now, so far into a conversation with God himself (consider that God has been suffering this weakness patiently, for this is a long conversation and Moses' slowness of speech must be making it drag on all the longer).

Why has Moses' weakness remained instead of being transformed by the powerful presence of God? We have seen from the beginning that God is not afraid of the mud. It's what he used to make Adam. It's what he looked past when fulfilling his promise to a man and woman who laughed at him. It is what he patiently tolerated in the patriarch Jacob, allowing him to retain a blessing that he received through deception and trickery. God transforms mud into mercy. This kind of mud constitutes the gems which God most prefers to magnify his presence. It is the earthen vessel which reveals a treasure.

A person's weakness tends to draw forth affection from us. In words of remembrance at funerals, it is often references to the weakness and foibles of the beloved deceased that draw forth laughter and tears. Somehow those weaknesses made the person more approachable and lovable. The weakness was somehow a prism through which the person's inherent goodness was more clearly evident, an opening through which his or her love was more easily received.

Recall that Saint Paul himself begged that his weakness be taken away, and Jesus responded, *My grace is sufficient for you, for power is made perfect in weakness* (2 Cor 12:9). God's response to Moses' complaint is similar: *It is I who will assist you in speaking and will teach you what you are to say* (Ex 4:12). God is not deterred by Moses' weakness in speech, but Moses' trust in God's promise is still not quite there. Moses recommends, *If you please, LORD, send someone else* (Ex 4:13). God has been patient with Moses to this point, but now he gets angry. Moses is questioning God's choice. Like Abraham and Sarah, he thinks God's promises are too great to reach fulfillment; and he doubts God's method of choosing frail flesh as the conduit of his divinity.

Yet God's patience perdures, and he allows Moses to take his well-spoken brother Aaron to accompany him. And then God tells Moses something quite amazing, *He shall be your spokesman; and you shall be as God to him* (Ex 4:16). Moses, a mere man, yes, that Moses, the one who is poor of speech, that's right, the one who killed a man and fled his country, he will be as God. And just in case we read that wrong, and would like to temper God's words a bit, God says it again. After Pharaoh rebuffs Moses' request to let the Hebrews go, and the Hebrews suffer for it, Moses again complains to God, *Since I am a poor speaker, how can it be that Pharaoh will listen to me?* and the Lord answers him, *I have made you as God to Pharaoh, and Aaron your brother shall act as your prophet* (Ex 6:30–7:1).

But wait, Moses is not only as God to Aaron and to Pharaoh. He is God's presence to the people. In his exchanges with Moses, God promises that he will save Israel from Egypt with his own outstretched hand or arm (Ex 3:20; 6:6; 7:5). After Pharaoh finally allows the Israelites to leave, he changes his mind and pursues them to the Red Sea. When they see the Egyptians at their heels, the people are greatly frightened and cry out to God. At this point God tells Moses, *"Why are you crying out to me? Tell the Israelites to go forward. And you, lift up your staff and, with hand outstretched over the sea, split the sea in two, that the Israelites may pass through it on dry land…." Then Moses stretched out his hand over the sea, and the* LORD *swept the sea with a strong east wind throughout the night and so turned it into dry land* (Ex 14:15-16, 21). God promised that his outstretched hand would save the Israelites, and at the crucial moment, God tells Moses to stretch out his own hand over the sea. God's hand and Moses' hand are one. God has willed that he would save the Israelites from Egypt through a man. The Church sees the Israelites' liberation from slavery in Egypt as a foreshadowing of the ultimate redemption wrought by Jesus. In the first case, it is an amazingly close cooperation, even an identification of God with Moses; in the case of Christ, the promise fulfilled, it is the Incarnation of God himself in human flesh.

As God promised the coming of Jesus in the Garden of Eden (Gn 3:15) with thinly veiled language, he will do the same during the sojourn of the Israelites in the desert. When they arrived at the desert of Sinai, God told Moses that he would come down on the mountain before the eyes of all the people. On that day, after God gave the Ten Commandments to Moses, *the peo-*

ple witnessed the thunder and lightning, the trumpet blast and the mountain smoking, [and] they all feared and trembled. So they took up a position much farther away and said to Moses, "You speak to us, and we will listen; but let not God speak to us, or we shall die" (Ex 20:18-19). Moses later reminds the people of the day they backed away from God in fear: *You said "Let us not again hear the voice of the LORD, our God, nor see this great fire any more, lest we die." And the LORD said to me, "This was well said. I will raise up for them a prophet like you from among their kinsmen, and will put my words into his mouth; he shall tell them all that I command him"* (Dt 18:16-18).

God knows that he is infinitely beyond us and so the manifestation of his greatness is too great for us. Backing away from thunder and lightning and smoke and fire is a normal human response. Moses is not afraid because he had come to know God over time, beginning with a small burning bush. God does not blame the people for backing away; he does not berate them for requesting that he speak to them through Moses (they were never afraid of

Moses—perhaps it had to do with that pesky and humiliating slowness of speech).

God completely agrees with the people's very human request. He commends them, *This was well said.* And he promises to send them a prophet from their own kinsmen. He does not want them to back away from him in fear. He wants to come close to them, like a mother hen *gather[ing] her brood under her wings* (Lk 13:34). Both Saint Peter and Saint Stephen will preach that the promised prophet is Jesus (Acts 3:22; 7:37) God is promising that he will come in the flesh. This is not only to fulfill the desire of the people, but to fulfill God's own desire. God does not will to be cold and distant; he is full of affection for his people. He does not want to remain a mountain away from us and watch Moses come close; he wants Emanuel, God with us.

He will not contend or cry out,/
nor will anyone hear his voice in the streets.
A bruised reed he will not break,
a smoldering wick he will not quench,

until he brings justice to victory.
   (Mt 12:19-20, cf. Is 42:2-3)

*Come to me, all you who labor and are bur-
dened, and I will give you rest. Take my yoke upon
you and learn from me, for I am meek and humble of heart; and you will find rest for yourselves.
For my yoke is easy, and my burden light.* (Mt
11:28-30)

God's Presence through a Human Family

A bit of background is needed to understand
the importance of David, a royal forerunner of
Christ the King.

What is called the period of the judges began
after the chosen people entered the Promised
Land. A judge was chosen directly by God from
among the people to lead them through a crisis.
It was not a hereditary succession, as in a kingly
line. Each judge would be chosen directly by
God, who himself remained the king of his chosen people. This required the people to trust that
God would raise up suitable leaders for them. This
period lasted until the end of the time that Sam-

uel was judging Israel. At that point, the elders of Israel asked Samuel, *Appoint a king over us, as other nations have, to judge us* (1 Sm 8:5). This request caused Samuel concern, and he prayed to God, who answered him, *Grant the people's every request. It is not you they reject, they are rejecting me as their king* (1 Sm 8:7).

God's assessment of their request is succinct and straightforward. They are asking for a human king, a king other than God, and thus they are rejecting him. They didn't even ask God to appoint the king; they asked Samuel. The rejection of God is also implied in their desire to be *as other nations*. They are the nation chosen by God; they are supposed to be exceptional among the nations. As the history of the kings plays out, God's granting of the people's request will itself be a chastisement of their rejection, for human kingship will lead to human corruption. But recall God's understanding of the request of the people at Sinai; he respected the humanity from which it came. At the culmination of this messy history, God will show understanding and mercy toward his people's desire for a human king.

Saul is chosen as the first king of Israel, but because of his disobedience, God rejects Saul and sends Samuel to the house of Jesse of Bethlehem. Saul would remain king until his death, but the Lord chose that the future line of kings would begin from one of Jesse's sons. Jesse presents seven sons to Samuel, but the Lord does not choose any of them. Samuel asks if there are others, and Jesse replies that his youngest son is out tending sheep. Samuel asks that he be summoned, and when David arrives the Lord commands Samuel to anoint him, and the Spirit of the Lord rushes upon him (1 Sm 16:1-13).

Once David was king and settled in his palace and the Lord had given him rest from his enemies, David decided that he should build a house for the Lord in which he would place the Ark of the Covenant. God intervened through Nathaniel the prophet to tell David that it was not for him to build a house for God. It was God who destroyed David's enemies; it would be God, instead, who would build a house for David. And then God made a promise to David, the importance of which cannot be overstated:

The LORD also reveals to you that he will establish a house for you.... I will raise up your heir after you, sprung from your loins, and I will make his kingdom firm. It is he who shall build a house for my name. And I will make his royal throne firm forever. I will be father to him, and he shall be a son to me.... Your house and your kingdom shall endure forever before me; your throne shall stand firm forever (2 Sm 7:11-14, 16).

The Davidic promise would be central for the chosen people's expectation of a Messiah who would come from the house of David, and this hope would be challenged in the succeeding generations. David's son and successor, King Solomon, would turn to false gods (1 Kgs 11:4-6). He had been warned that, should he do so, he would lose the land and the temple (1 Kgs 9:3-9), but not the kingdom, because that was promised forever. Under the foolish rule of Solomon's son, Rehoboam, the northern region of the kingdom seceded. God instructed the southern region not to fight against their brother Israelites, for he was allowing this to happen. There were now two kingdoms: Judah in the south, under Davidic kings, and Israel in the north, which had rebelled against David's house (1 Kgs 12:16-19). The northern kingdom was conquered by Assyria in 721 B.C., and its subjects disappear from history, the lost tribes of Israel. The southern kingdom fell to Babylon around 586 B.C. This exile would have been a very confusing time. God had promised to David that his kingdom would last forever. What did this promise mean in a time when the kingdom seemed irretrievably lost?

Years later, Cyrus, king of Persia, conquered Babylon and allowed the exiles to return to their land. But when they returned they no longer had their own kingdom. They existed mostly under foreign powers, ultimately the Roman Empire, at which point descendants of David no longer lived as royalty. One of them was a carpenter from Nazareth.

With this history in mind, we can understand the significance of the references to David that accompanied the announcements of the Birth of Jesus:

In the sixth month, the angel Gabriel was sent from God to a town of Galilee called Nazareth, to a virgin betrothed to a man named Joseph, of the house of David, and the virgin's name was Mary. And coming to her, he said, "Hail, favored one! The Lord is with you." But she was greatly troubled at what was said and pondered what sort of greeting this might be. Then the angel said to her, "Do not be afraid, Mary, for you have found favor with God. Behold, you will conceive in your womb and bear a son, and you shall name him Jesus. He will be great and will be called Son of the Most High, and the Lord God will give him the throne of David his father, and he will rule over the house of Jacob forever, and of his kingdom there will be no end." But Mary said to the angel, "How can this be, since I have no relations with a man?" And the angel said to her in reply, "The holy Spirit will come upon you, and the power of the Most High will overshadow you. Therefore the child to be born will be called holy, the Son of God. And behold, Elizabeth, your relative, has also conceived a son in her old age, and this is the sixth month for her who was called barren; for nothing will be impossible for God." Mary said, "Behold, I am the handmaid of the Lord. May it be done to me according to your word." (Lk 1:26-38)

The angel of the Lord appeared to him in a dream and said, "Joseph, son of David, do not be afraid to take Mary your wife into your home. For it is through the holy Spirit that this child has been conceived in her. She will bear a son and you are to name him Jesus, because he will save his people from their sins." All this took place to fulfill what the Lord had said through the prophet:
"Behold, the virgin shall be with child
and bear a son,
and they shall name him Emmanuel,"
which means "God is with us." (Mt 1:20-23)

The angel said to them, "Do not be afraid; for behold, I proclaim to you good news of great joy that will be for all the people. For today in the city of David a savior has been born for you who is Messiah and Lord. And this will be a sign for you: you will find an infant wrapped in swaddling clothes and lying in a manger." (Lk 2:10-12)

Through Joseph, Jesus is an heir in the house of David. Gabriel makes specific reference to the Davidic promise at the Annunciation to Mary. Joseph and Mary must go to Bethlehem at the time of the census because Joseph, being of the house of David, must go to his ancestral town. The angels' appearance to shepherds near Bethlehem also recalls David, who was tending sheep in Bethlehem when the Lord summoned him through Samuel to be anointed king.

Ultimately, how did God respond to the rejection of the people who asked Samuel for a human king? He gave them everything.

In Jesus, God is once again their king; and in Jesus they have a human king. As an heir in the line of David, he is the King whose kingdom will last forever. If we are honest with ourselves, we can understand the people's desire for a king that they can see and touch. It is a very human request. God affirms and responds to our humanity...with his humanity.

More tortuous than all else is the human heart, beyond remedy; who can understand it? (Jer

17:9). God understands it, and the Son of God became man to remedy it.

Almost as tortuous as the human heart was the history of the kings brought about by the people's request. Since God no longer chose the kings directly, allowing succession by heredity just like other nations, he raised up prophets to warn the kingdoms of their impending fall and to comfort the southern tribes during their exile in Babylon. The greatest comfort came in the form of a promise, the promise of him who is to come: Jesus, who fulfills and surpasses every one of the ancient promises. He is more than a prophet, more than a king, a Messiah even greater than what they could have expected; he is God himself, the Word made flesh who dwells among us.

But you, Bethlehem-Ephrathah,
too small to be among the clans of Judah,
From you shall come forth for me
one who is to be ruler in Israel;
Whose origin is from of old,
from ancient times.

(Therefore the Lord will give them up,
until the time
when she who is to give birth has borne,
And the rest of his brethren shall return
to the children of Israel.)
He shall stand firm and shepherd his flock
by the strength of the LORD,
in the majestic name of the LORD, *his God;*
And they shall remain, for now his greatness
shall reach to the ends of the earth;
he shall be peace. (Mic 5:1-4)

The LORD *spoke to Ahaz: Ask for a sign from the* LORD, *your God; let it be deep as the nether world, or high as the sky! But Ahaz answered, "I will not ask! I will not tempt the* LORD!" *Then he said: Listen, O house of David! Is it not enough for you to weary men, must you also weary my God? Therefore the Lord himself will give you this sign: the virgin shall be with child, and bear a son, and shall name him Immanuel.* (Is 7:10-14)

The people who walked in darkness
have seen a great light;

upon those who dwelt in the land of gloom
a light has shone.
For a child is born to us, a son is given us;
upon his shoulder dominion rests.
They name him Wonder-Counselor, God-Hero,
Father-Forever, Prince of Peace.
His dominion is vast
and forever peaceful,
From David's throne, and over his kingdom,
which he confirms and sustains
By judgment and justice,
both now and forever.
    (Is 9:1, 5-6)

*On that day the L*ORD *will shield the inhabitants*
of Jerusalem, and the weakling among them shall
be like David on that day, and the house of David
*godlike, like the angel of the L*ORD *before them. On*
that day I will seek the destruction of all nations
that come against Jerusalem.

I will pour out on the house of David and on the
inhabitants of Jerusalem a spirit of grace and peti-
tion, and they shall look on him whom they have

thrust through, and they shall mourn for him as one
mourns for an only son, and they will grieve over
him as one grieves over a firstborn. (Zec 12:8-10)

Behold, the days are coming, says the LORD,
when I will raise up a righteous shoot to David;
As king he shall reign and govern wisely,
he shall do what is just and right in the land.
In his days Judah shall be saved,
Israel shall dwell in security.
This is the name they give him:
"The LORD our justice."
    (Jer 23:5-6)

PART II

EMMANUEL,
GOD WITH US

CHAPTER 4

⸎⸎⸎⸎

The Word becomes Flesh

What Were the Disciples Looking For?

Jesus didn't *appear* human, he really *became* human. He lived in a particular place at a particular time. It seems, unsurprisingly, that he spoke with the accent of Galilee from which he came (Mt 26:73). From the lack of reference in the Gospels, we can surmise that from childhood until he began his public ministry his life was ordinary.

In fact, the day he met his first disciples (Jn 1:35-51) he was so much like anyone else of that place and time that he had to be pointed out by John the Baptist.

John and Andrew were disciples of John the Baptist, who, with his eccentric garb, strange diet, and aggressive preaching, was, at that time, much more conspicuous than Jesus. (His garments, by the way, are the same as those worn by the prophet Elijah, who was prophesied to come before the day of the Lord, see Mk 1:6; 2 Kgs 1:8; and Mal 3:23). One day, when Andrew and John were with John the Baptist, he pointed to a man walking by and said, *Behold, the Lamb of God.* Hindsight is 20/20, so we know what that title means: Jesus is the fulfillment of the Passover lamb that was sacrificed to save the firstborn son from death. What would John and Andrew have made of this title? They had simply come to trust John the Baptist enough to follow after the man he indicated. Jesus kept walking, and they followed behind. At a certain point he turned and asked them, *What are you looking for?*

He was fully human. Turning around to two strangers following you to ask what they want is a fully human response. He is fully divine. Is God in there somewhere? I find it very interesting that the first words of Jesus to these first disciples were not *Repent,* which they would have heard from John the Baptist often enough; nor *Follow me,* which they were doing already, but *What are you looking for?*

What were they looking for? If they were disciples of a man like John the Baptist they must have been hoping for something. Perhaps the Messiah? Some wondered if John the Baptist might be he, though he denied it. If they followed John the Baptist, believing he was a prophet, then they were seeking God. I previously stated that God is Infinite Being and we are infinite need; our limitless need is the perfect echo of his Limitless Being. Is Jesus addressing himself to their infinite desire, the image of his Father in them? Is he inviting them to discover that he is what they are looking for? It is interesting that John's Gospel begins with *What are you looking for?* and leads to the question *Whom are you looking for?* which Jesus addresses to Mary Magdalene as she is seeking him outside his tomb (Jn 20:15). In line with the prophets before him, John the Baptist pointed his disciples toward God. As the forerunner of all Christians, he has pointed these disciples toward Jesus.

John and Andrew asked Jesus where he was staying, and he invited them to stay with him that day. In his Gospel, John recalls the time; it was about four o'clock in the afternoon. When they returned, we don't know how many hours later, they were certain that they had *found the Messiah*, so certain that Andrew said as much to his brother Peter (Jn 1:41).

What could have happened during their time with Jesus that would have given them such certainty? I don't know. But if I trust the Gospel I know what didn't happen. Jesus did not perform a miracle for them, because this is John's Gospel and John tells us that Jesus' first sign was to change water to wine at the wedding at Cana, which occurred after this encounter. That there was no miracle meant that there was something so exceptional in his humanity itself that it was reasonable for them to trust him. Mark tells us that the first thing that astonished the first hearers of Jesus was that *he taught them as one having authority and not as the scribes* (Mk 1:22). The scribes presumably spoke about God; they knew things about him from their knowledge of Scripture. But Jesus doesn't only know *about* God; he knows God, like a son knows his father. His familiarity with God must not have come off as academic or formally religious; there must have been something astoundingly natural about it. And he not only spoke of his Father, but the Father was somehow visible in him. Recall what he said to Philip, *Whoever has seen me has seen the Father* (Jn 14:9). We have our parents' mannerisms; it's just the way it is. Even in his humanity, Jesus is somehow reminiscent of the Father. Fully human, so they comprehended the words he was saying, and fully divine—there was something amazing, more profound, more visceral than his words, something they could not put their finger on, but was most definitely there.

I was once studying this passage with a group of high school students, and I asked them what John and Andrew might have done with Jesus that day. One young woman thought it might have been like a Communion and Liberation "high school vacation," which she had been to the previous summer. It had been for her a pivotal discovery that Christ is real, and really present. I asked if she thought Jesus played slip and slide on a big tarp with John and Andrew, as we had done at the vacation, and perhaps roasted marshmallows with them late into the evening while singing all kinds of songs. She laughed and said no, not those particular things, but there must have been the same exceptionality present that so moved her on the vacation. "I think John didn't tell us what they did," she concluded, "because it is not something you can explain. You have to 'Come and See.' John didn't tell us because he is inviting us to come and see and discover it for ourselves."

"'Come and See,'" Msgr. Giussani would say, "This is the formula, *the* Christian formula. This is the Christian method: 'Come and See.'"[4]

What did the demons want?

As we saw in the first chapter, the angels rejoiced at the coming of the Son of God in the flesh; the demons, not so much. Mark's Gospel indicates that they put up their resistance to Jesus very early in his ministry. In that same synagogue in Capernaum where his listeners were astonished at his authority, a man possessed by a demon interrupted and screamed, *I know who you are—the Holy One of God!* (Mk 1:24). That evening, Mark writes, *he drove out many demons, not permitting them to speak because they knew him* (Mk 1:34). The demons' strategy is to cry out the true identity of Jesus. Telling the truth is not what we would expect of demons; but it is a clever and insidious method of resistance. It aims straight for Jesus' humanity, trying to intercept the Incarnate Word as he courts our humanity.

Let me offer an example. A young man goes off to college. In his first semester there is a girl on campus that he greatly admires, but has found no way to approach. Before Thanksgiving break he posts a notice that he has space available in his car, should anyone need to go to back to his hometown. Lo and behold, she responds! He didn't know that she came from the next town over. They take the long drive home, let's say four or five hours. After dropping her off, he arrives at his house and bursts through the door, proclaiming, "Mom, Dad, I just spent the day with the girl I am going to marry!" They calm him down and he explains the beautiful girl, the car ride, and everything.

At the end of Thanksgiving break, her parents drop her off at his house for the ride back. As the college boy and girl are in the driveway packing the car, the boy's little brother, let's say...seventh grade?...emerges from the house with a big smile on his face and calls out "Hey, is this the girl you said you're gonna marry?" To say the very least, the young man would like to silence his brother, and not permit him to speak. For his brother has cornered him into a very awkward ride back to college.

All the little brother did was tell the truth. But blurting out the truth at that moment was insidious. It did not respect the dynamic of the relationship. For the young man would, perhaps, on the way back, have asked the girl if she would like to get together for coffee, or dinner, or a movie. Maybe things would work out and there would be a second date. Maybe they would become exclusive. Maybe in a few years, after they graduate, he would propose and perhaps, having had time to come to know and love him, she would say yes.

Jesus did not present himself on day one as the Son of God. People would likely have backed away and thought he was crazy. They saw something exceptional in him, but it would take time to come to believe that the exceptionality was due to the very presence of God. It would take time even for his closest disciples to recognize his divinity. It would require time spent together, so that certainty could grow. Just as each partner of a couple likely thinks about marriage long before speaking of it, Jesus, the Bridegroom of the Church, gave his disciples time before explicitly claiming to be God. In many ways he indicated his divinity indirectly. For instance, when a paralytic was placed before him he forgave his sins, which only God can do. When he was challenged about that, he healed the man in order to verify that he indeed possessed the authority to forgive sins (Mk 2:5-12).

Jesus respects our humanity, our need for time. He wants his disciples to believe in him, ultimately, because each one has come to that truth himself, through life lived with him, through a series of confirmations that deepen conviction. When John the Baptist pointed to Jesus as the Lamb of God, John and Andrew didn't ask for an explanation; they followed him and came to believe themselves that he is the Messiah, because of the time they spent with him. Later on, Samaritans who come to Jesus because of the Samaritan woman will tell her, *We no longer believe because of your word; for we have heard for ourselves, and we know that this is truly the savior of the world* (Jn 4:42). Recall that Moses was not afraid of the fire and thunder at Sinai as the others were; he had first encountered God in a small burning bush, and saw that the bush was not destroyed by the fire, and conversed with God and followed him over time, and trusted and stumbled and trusted again, and the relationship was deepened.

The demons want to sabotage this human path. Perhaps in their arrogance they despise our need for time, our need for reassurance, our hesitating and faltering and returning again to follow in fits and starts. Jesus loves this about us. He looks upon our humanity with the utmost tenderness. He is so attracted by our humanity that he wants to share it with us.

The angels rejoiced immediately at the revelation of the Incarnation (and the demons resisted immediately). The shepherds needed time; they needed to make a journey. Even Mary needed to ponder the mystery in her heart. We need time. Humans need time. God has become human; he accompanies us in time.

Others Experienced the Uniqueness of His Presence

The exceptionality of Jesus was notable to anyone who encountered him, not just those who were already seeking God, like John and Andrew. In taking flesh, God doesn't wait for us to seek him; he makes himself present and bumps into us. Even if a certain kind of religious formalism might get in the way of being open to Jesus; it does not stop the person from recognizing a very different humanity.

Many religious leaders considered Jesus to be dangerous precisely because they saw something about him that was attractive to so many. The mercy which drew sinners to Jesus would be often scandalize the publicly and respectably religious. The Pharisee Nicodemus was curious about Jesus, but visited him at night for fear of the Jews (Jn 3:1-21). Similarly, Joseph of Arimathea was a secret disciple who would only have the strength to "go public" after Jesus died on the cross (Jn 19:38-42).

In the case of the rich young man who came to Jesus, we do not know if he ever became a disciple. Mark tells us that he knelt before Jesus and asked, *Good teacher, what must I do to inherit eternal life?* Jesus answered, *Why do you call me good? No one is good but God alone* (Mk 10:17-18). Is Jesus calling the man to consider a more radical question than what he has to do? Why, instead, is he kneeling in front of a carpenter from Nazareth? In Jesus' disconcerting response it seems that he is provoking the man to wonder about what has drawn him to Jesus in the first place. The goodness this man sees in a carpenter from Nazareth, who is the most authoritative teacher he has ever encountered, is God. The rich man goes away because he has many possessions; he goes away sad because, as attached as he is to his possessions and as great as they may be, it is clear that in Jesus he has met something greater.

If I begin from my own unaided efforts, of course I will be sad, because my efforts falter. But in the Incarnation God has turned everything around. The energy to follow Jesus does not come from my willpower; the source of that energy is the attraction to the Person of Jesus himself. Msgr. Giussani calls this the "overturning of the religious method." He writes that because of the Incarnation our relationship with God "will no longer be based on human effort, the fruit of man's construction or imagination...or on waiting for something absent. Instead it will mean coming up against something present...the experience of a present, an encounter."[5]

Because of a big conversion he had in college, a seminary classmate of mine concluded that he should become a priest in order to thank Jesus or somehow pay him back. After a couple of years of formation, he noticed a joy that the other seminarians had that he did not. Another seminarian told him that when he spoke of vocation he used the word "should" quite a bit. This other seminarian's own personal experience was that his joy in following a vocation to the priesthood arose from a clear sense that this path held out a promise for his happiness, a promise whose fulfillment was unfolding day by day, even if it included sacrifices. My classmate instead was beginning from what he should do, like the rich young man. But he had not arranged his encounter with Jesus in college, it came as a surprise; so why would he think that once he followed Jesus it would be up to him to decide how that following would play out? He followed Jesus out of the seminary, became involved in a lay community, pursued his interest in music and teaching, and is now a very happy husband and father. Jesus did not become incarnate in his life in college only to abandon him. Christ was incarnate in his friends in the seminary, in the friends he met after the seminary, and, in a sacramental way, in his wife.

John wrote, *In this is love: not that we have loved God, but that he loved us and sent his Son as expiation for our sins* (1 Jn 4:10). We act like the rich young man when we begin from what we do. Instead, when we are poor in spirit enough to recognize that God has taken the initiative in our existence and in our conversion by sending his Son, then we proceed with the joyful wonder and attentiveness of children who are amazed at what the Father has done. My classmate paid painstaking attention to what Christ was making evident in his life, and was ultimately led to his vocation. The rich man is sad because he is not faithful to his attraction to Jesus of Nazareth. To the Incarnation he has preferred to hold on to his possessions and search for a religious formula.

The objectivity of the enigmatic presence that Jesus bears is perhaps nowhere more evident than in his encounter with Pontius Pilate, as recounted in the Gospel of John (Jn 18:28–19:22). Pilate wondered why the Jewish leaders delivered this man up to him. He assumed it was an offense against their religion and so wanted to give Jesus back to them to judge him themselves. The Jewish leaders responded, *We do not have the right to execute anyone.* Pilate may have been a bit taken aback by this; what could this man have done that deserved death?

Pilate went back to the prisoner and asked if he were the king of the Jews. Jesus turned the tables and interrogated Pilate, asking if he recognized this on his own or because he had been told. Pilate was definitely taken aback by this and reminded Jesus just who had been handed over to whom. A conversation ensued about the nature of Jesus' mysterious kingship. What was obvious to Pilate was that this prisoner was exceptional. Pilate even asked him, *What is truth?* Was he approaching discipleship? At the very least he was certain that there was no guilt in Jesus. He tried to release him, but the Jewish leaders asked him to release Barabbas instead.

So Pilate took Jesus, whom he believed to be innocent, and had him scourged in order to appease those who had handed him over. Pilate was a politician, after all, but he clearly did not want to be involved in Jesus' death. The truth he saw in Jesus challenged his political cynicism. When the scourging was not enough for the Jewish leaders and they still called for Jesus' crucifixion, Pilate lost his composure for a moment—*Take him yourselves and crucify him. I find no guilt in him*—thus recommending an illegal act. The Jewish leaders responded, *We have a law, and according to that law he ought to die, because he made himself the Son of God*. And John writes that *when Pilate heard this statement, he became even more afraid*.

He became even more afraid. Why? Once he heard this lofty claim you would expect he might laugh, and decide that Jesus was crazy. But no, he was more afraid. This tells us first that Pilate was afraid already, that there was an awesome authority he saw in Jesus that he had not seen before. And Pilate moved in circles where he would have encountered men with great authority. Secondly, because of his short but profound encounter with Jesus, once he heard the claim regarding *the Son of God*, it didn't seem crazy to Pilate, but quite possible. That he took this claim seriously is evidenced in his next question to Jesus, *Where are you from?*

As the conversation continued, Jesus told Pilate, *the one who handed me over to you has the greater sin.* The Gospel tells us that *consequently, Pilate tried to release him.* Jesus' claim that those responsible for his death would incur sin rang true to Pilate, not only because of the words, but because of the enigmatic gravitas of Jesus himself. The man who earlier asked *What is truth* has begun to discover Who is Truth. When he brought Jesus out he seated him on the judge's bench. The iconography Pilate provided was Jesus sitting in judgment while he observed the final exchange between the Jewish leaders and Pilate.

Tragically, Pilate gave in and handed Jesus over to death. But the inscription he placed over Jesus read *Jesus the Nazorean, the King of the Jews.* The leaders were upset by this and complained to Pilate. Pilate's response was direct and simple, *What I have written, I have written.*

Pilate was not looking for God that day. A scuffle with the Jewish leaders over laws he did not understand was likely the last thing he was looking for. But the prisoner he met that day was unlike anything he could ever have expected, and not something that he would soon forget. Whether Pilate became a disciple later in life is debated. But the exceptionality of that encounter is undeniable.

Even the hatred and violence that surrounded his death could not obscure the goodness in Jesus, which could only come from God. Mark recounts for us that *When the centurion who stood facing him saw how he breathed his last he said, "Truly this man was the Son of God"* (Mk 15:39).

Was that centurion a spiritual man, looking for enlightenment that day? Or was he just doing his job? This probably wasn't the first time his tour of duty involved guarding the crosses of those to be executed. What might the typical behavior of the crucified be? Perhaps weeping and begging for his life; or begging to be killed quickly and to be spared torturously slow death of the cross. Another type of personality might spew every possible curse against anyone and everyone he blamed for putting him where he was.

What did the centurion see happening as Jesus died? He saw him praying for those who had plotted his death, and forgiving those who were taunting him even as they were doing it. He saw his concern for his Mother. He might have heard him promising paradise to the repentant thief crucified next to him. Finally, he saw Jesus commend his Spirit to the Father and breathe his last.

From what Mark's Gospel tells us, it was not miracles or preaching that brought that centurion to recognize Jesus' divinity on that Good Friday; it was seeing the unprecedented way that this crucified prisoner lived his final hours which brought that guard to confess Jesus as the Son of God.

Now since the children share in blood and flesh, he likewise shared in them, that through death he might destroy the one who has the power of death, that is, the devil, and free those who through fear of death had been subject to slavery all their life. Surely he did not help angels but rather the descendants of Abraham; therefore, he had to become like his brothers in every way, that he might be a merciful and faithful high priest before God to expiate the sins of the people. (Heb 2:14-17)

CHAPTER 5

༺❀❀❀༻

The Incarnation Is Magnified through the Disciples

Authority Given to the Apostles and Disciples

Very early in his public ministry, Jesus calls disciples to himself. We considered the first disciples in the previous chapter. But, after some time, Jesus chooses twelve from among his disciples to become Apostles. Mark tells us that Jesus appointed them to be Apostles so *that they might be with him and he might send them forth to preach* (Mk 3:14). It is important to note that they must first be with him, not merely be trained or instructed by him, but be with him. The source of their preaching will not be a rule of life that they have learned or a philosophy that they have mastered. Their preaching will arise organically from their relationship with Jesus. All that they say and do will be generated and enlivened by that relationship, just as all that Jesus says and does is an expression of his relationship with the Father.

What prompted Jesus' desire that his authority shine forth not only through his own flesh but also through the frail flesh of the Apostles? Matthew tells us that it was his pity for the crowds, who *were troubled and abandoned, like sheep without a shepherd* (Mt 9:36). Jesus wants to be present to everyone, but he has become human, which means that he has subjected himself to the limits of space and time to which humans are subject. His heart was moved by the crowds, who needed to meet God's presence in a human face. And so to offer such an encounter to as many as possible, he summoned Apostles from among his disciples. As the Father sent him, so he would send them. As the Father bestowed his authority on Jesus, Jesus would bestow his authority on the Apostles (Mt 10:1). He commanded them to do the very same things that he was doing: *Cure the sick, raise the dead, cleanse lepers, drive out demons* (Mt 10:8). In a mysterious way, they would be the presence of Jesus in the towns and villages where they were sent.

Luke recounts the call of the Twelve as well, but he also speaks of Jesus sending out not just the twelve Apostles, but seventy-two disciples. These, too, were commanded to *cure the sick* in his name and proclaim that *the kingdom of God is at hand* (Lk 10:9). In addition, Luke notes that Jesus sent these disciples not alone, but in pairs. The disciples also need Jesus in the flesh, and as they are sent away from Jesus to the towns, two by two, each would serve as a reminder of Christ's presence to the other.

When the seventy-two returned rejoicing that even the demons were subject to them because of Jesus' name, Jesus rejoiced in the Holy Spirit and praised the Father for revealing himself through these disciples. Then Jesus warned the seventy-two, *do not rejoice because the spirits are subject to you, but rejoice because your names are written in heaven* (Lk 10:20). If they become fascinated with the power they have been given and forget that it comes from God's presence within them, they will become prideful and lose their joy. Only if the source of their joy is belonging to the Father through the Son in the Holy Spirit will they remain humble and effective witnesses that God is with us.

It is significant that Jesus rejoiced *in the holy Spirit* (Lk 10:21) when he saw that his presence had been multiplied through his disciples and his divinity had been revealed in their humanity. For it is the Holy Spirit who makes Jesus present in the flesh. Recall at the Annunciation, when the Blessed Virgin Mary asked how it could be that the Son of the Most High would take flesh in her womb, and Gabriel replied, *The holy Spirit will come upon you* (Lk 1:35). The Holy Spirit came upon Mary, and the Word became flesh. At the epiclesis of the Mass, the priest begs that the Holy Spirit come upon the gifts of bread and wine so that they may become the Body and Blood of Christ. When the Holy Spirit comes, Jesus becomes physically present in the Eucharist. At Pentecost, the Apostles were completely transformed into other Christs by the descent of the Holy Spirit, and thus the Church, the Body of Christ in the world, was born. The seventy-two disciples somehow extending the presence of Jesus to the towns into which they went was a kind of prophecy of what was to be. Jesus rejoiced that the Father had willed to pour out the Spirit so abundantly that the Word made flesh could be encountered by every person to whom the Son wishes to reveal the Father (Lk 10:21-22).

Jesus seemingly referred to this mystery again in the Gospel of John when he said to the Apostles at the Last Supper, *Amen, Amen, I say to you, whoever believes in me will do the works that I do, and will do greater ones than these, because I am going to the Father…. And I will ask the Father, and he will give you another Advocate to be with you always, the Spirit of truth* (Jn 14:12, 16). How can believers do greater works than Jesus? When Jesus, who is fully divine, brings God's healing to the world it is wondrous; but when an ordinary person, a sinner like you or me, becomes the bearer of God's healing presence through belonging to Christ, it is even more unexpected. God's generosity and desire to be with us extends beyond the time and place of the first coming of Christ in the flesh. Jesus doesn't just come, he promises to remain. He doesn't want to work alone; he wants to work with us and through us, in a cooperation and communion that we could never have asked for or imagined.

When Jesus sent his Apostles out he told them, *Do not go into pagan territory, or enter a Samaritan town. Go rather to the lost sheep of the house of Israel* (Mt 10:5-6).

As Jesus chose Jewish Apostles to be his presence among the Jews, he will choose a Samaritan and a Gentile to make his presence known in Samaria and in Gentile territory.

The Samaritan Woman

To appreciate the dialogue between Jesus and the Samaritan woman we should revisit the Old Testament history of the kings and the secession of the north, which resulted in two separate kingdoms. Jerusalem was the capital of the southern kingdom of Judah, and Samaria was the capital of the northern kingdom of Israel. The northern kings, who were not of the line of David, established separate shrines in the north as alternate worship sites to Jerusalem. The northerners would thus become suspect in regard to their faithfulness as chosen people of God. Assyria conquered Israel about 135 years before Judah fell to Babylon. The Assyrian method was to deport much of the newly conquered population to different parts of its empire, and then repopulate that land with peoples from other regions. Thus the northern tribes emigrated and apparently assimilated to the point where they were no longer recognizable as God's chosen people, i.e., the lost tribes of Israel. The remnant of the Israelites left in the northern kingdom would have had little choice but to intermarry with the resettled Gentiles.

Thus, the Samaritans at the time of Jesus still claimed as their ancestors the Israelites of the north. The Jews, however, question the Samaritans' status as chosen people. Whatever "chosen" blood they had was derived from ancestors who had seceded from the Davidic kingdom, and even that was likely adulterated by generations of intermarriage with Gentiles. When the Jews returned from their Babylonian exile and were rebuilding the Temple, the Samaritans offered to help, with the claim, *We seek your God just as you do* (Ezr 4:2). The Jews responded, *It is not your responsibility to build with us a house for our God, but we alone must build it for the LORD, the God of Israel* (Ezr 4:3). The Samaritans saw themselves as belonging to God's chosen people, but the Jews did not.

Luke recounts an episode when a Samaritan town did not welcome Jesus and his disciples as they were passing through, because they were journeying to Jerusalem. James and John asked Jesus if they should call down fire from heaven to consume the Samaritans, but Jesus rebuked them (Lk 9:51-56).

In Jn 8:48, the Jewish leaders attempt to insult Jesus by asking, *Are we not right in saying that you are a Samaritan and are possessed?* Perhaps they invoked "Samaritan" as an epithet because Jesus grew up in Nazareth, which had been part of the northern kingdom, and he likely spoke with a northern accent as Peter did (Mt 26:73). Interestingly, Jesus limits his response to, *I am not possessed* (Jn 8:49), thereby rejecting the inference of "Samaritan" as inherently insulting and thus refusing to distance himself from any group of people. Jesus is more explicit about his openness toward Samaritans in the famous parable of the Good Samaritan (Lk 10:30-37).

When Jesus and his disciples passed through the Samaritan town of Sychar, he decided to rest at what was called Jacob's well at about noon, and sent his disciples into town to buy food (Jn 4). Quite strange for a man to rest at a well at the hottest part of the day when he has no bucket.

And then one lone woman approached. Quite strange for a woman to come to the well at noon, when the usual time would be in the morning or evening, when it would be easier to carry the heavy load of water at a cooler time of day. But this woman likely preferred to be alone rather than suffer rejection or insult from townspeople who knew her sad past and her scandalous present. Her solitude was her defense.

She was probably surprised to see a Jewish man sitting there. She may have thought that she could still fetch her water and not be disturbed, because a Jewish man would not normally speak to a Samaritan woman. She would have to suffer nothing more than awkward silence; and, having been sent away by five husbands, she had surely suffered worse than that. But Jesus broke the silence and began to breach her defenses: *Give me a drink.*

Note that Jesus did not say "please." He is not being tender to this woman, as he was to the woman caught in adultery or the woman who washed his feet with her hair. He loves each of us uniquely, as a parent has a particular love for each child. He respects and responds to our history, our temperament, our wounds. A woman rejected by five husbands, who has so given up on herself that she is willing to live outside of marriage with a sixth, is not likely a woman who trusts tenderness from a man. And so Jesus was direct, even blunt.

She responded immediately: *How can you, a Jew, ask me, a Samaritan woman, for a drink?* She could have ignored him and walked away, but she answered right back. She was not afraid of him, and perhaps she was no longer particularly respectful of any man.

If you knew the gift of God and who is saying to you, "Give me a drink," you would have asked him and he would have given you living water.

When he called himself *gift of God* she likely thought he was referring to the fact that he was a Jew. She reminded him that he didn't have a bucket and thus challenged his claim that he could acquire living water. She added, *Are you greater than our father Jacob, who gave us this cistern and drank from it himself...?* She asserted to this "gift of God" that she too is a descendant of Jacob, a member of the chosen people.

The conversation, or bantering, continued. This itself is interesting. She could have left at any moment. If she walked away from a man who rudely disregarded social mores no one would blame her. But she stayed. There was something interesting about this strange Jewish man. He also stayed. He was not averse to speaking with her. In fact, he wasn't merely bantering, but was taking her quite seriously.

At some point, she took him seriously enough to ask for the living water he spoke about. He told her to call her husband and come back, to which she replied, *I do not have a husband.*

Jesus abruptly retorted, *You are right in saying, "I do not have a husband." For you have had five husbands, and the one you have now is not your husband. What you have said is true.*

Why did Jesus blurt out her deepest shame? He must have known those words would hurt her. But he was methodically breaking through the hardness of her heart.

Her misleading response was to put up a facade of respectability. Jesus tore it down as soon as she erected it. He had no interest in her attempt to "measure up." He didn't come to save her façade, but to bring salvation to her very core, to resurrect the infinite need for love which she had entombed in her defenses.

Her next defense was to return to the religion question, *Our ancestors worshiped on this mountain; but you people say that the place to worship is Jerusalem.* Jesus took down this façade as well: *You people worship what you do not understand; we worship what we understand, because salvation is from the Jews.* As if to tell her, "You want to use belonging to the chosen people as your measure? If you subject yourself to that measure, you won't measure up either." Jesus was not rejecting her; he was rejecting her attempt to "measure up."

He then proclaimed to her, *The hour is coming, and is now here, when true worshipers will worship the Father in Spirit and truth; and indeed the Father seeks such people to worship him.*

Having been stripped of her defenses, how could she respond to words she probably did not even understand? All she had left was the cry of her heart, *I know that the Messiah is coming, the one called the Anointed; when he comes, he will tell us everything.* Something at the depth of her being knows that the Messiah is coming for her. Whether she be "respectable" or not, whether "chosen" or not. Something in her knows.

This cry was not a façade, but the first true defense she expressed—she was defending her humanity. She was faithfully uttering what God had written in her heart, that which she had not dared to utter to anyone; for such an admission leaves you vulnerable, and such vulnerability had become impossible for her after so much hurt...until this man, who waited for her at the well.

And with this cry, Jesus found the treasure for which he was digging. He set free the cry to which he is the Answer: *I know that the Messiah is coming...she cried....*

I am he, the one who is speaking with you.

Could this man really be the Messiah? This was not a Messiah of power and fury. This was a Jewish man who looked like any other. But this Jewish man was sitting at a well in Samaria, waiting for her. He sent all of his disciples to buy food, because he likely knew that she would not approach if there were a group of men there. She might have been afraid. One lone man at the well? Nothing to be afraid of.

Let's go back to Jesus' blurting of her shame. It was hurtful, but necessary. He could not allow her to walk away from that well thinking, "he seems to take me seriously, he seems to be concerned for me, but if he really knew about me...." If he didn't reveal that he knew her shame, then his love would not have pierced her defenses. Her parched heart would still thirst for the living water that he was waiting at that well to give her.

Once when I was teaching this passage to high school students, a young man interrupted the reading of the passage and said, "He's talking to her like a Father; my father is sometimes harsh and direct at me like that, but I know it's because he loves me." The Samaritan woman has met the face of the Father in Jesus. She has seen in him a love that is truer than any love, or façade of love, that she has experienced before.

When the disciples returned, the woman ran into town and cried out to the townspeople, *Come see a man who told me everything I have done. Could he possibly be the Messiah?*

What a strange spectacle she must have been. The townspeople must have known her past. Why would she be happy to have someone recount it back to her? But her joy was genuine and infectious. Because of her, many townspeople came to see Jesus and began to believe in him.

The woman at the well in Samaria was a better witness to Jesus than Jesus himself could have been in that Samaritan town. Her townspeople shared with her the long history of animosity between Samaritans and Jews. How could Jesus bridge such a longstanding rift? Through one of their own.

The woman at the well had a sketchy past, but the townspeople knew her. It is perhaps because they knew her well that they were so surprised by her transformation. Whether or not they had taken her seriously, the new life they saw in her could not be dismissed. They were curious, and open, to the only explanation she could give, a Jewish man at the well. *Could he possibly be the Messiah?*

Jesus, in some sense, had taken flesh in the new life that radiated from the beloved woman of Samaria.

The Incarnation will know no bounds. The Word made flesh will seek to bridge every chasm. Person by person, face by face, heart by heart.

I will give you a new heart, and place a new spirit within you, taking from your bodies your stony hearts and giving you natural hearts. (Ez 36:26)

The LORD, your God, will circumcise your hearts and the hearts of your descendants, that you may love the LORD, your God, with all your heart and all your soul, and so may live. (Dt 30:6)

The Healed Gentile Prepares the Way for Jesus' Return

At some point in his ministry, Jesus proposed to his disciples to cross to the other side of the Sea of Galilee to Gentile territory (Mk 4:35-41). It was during this crossing that a storm arose that was so violent that the disciples thought it would kill them. In their terror they awakened Jesus, who commanded *Quiet! Be still!* and the wind ceased and was replaced by a great calm. Who was Jesus commanding? Was the power of evil upset that Jesus was going into pagan territory? The Messiah would not be satisfied with saving Jews and Samaritans; the Word made flesh wanted to bring his presence everywhere. He would accept the limits of being human, but would not suffer any limits on the salvation he came to bring.

When they arrived at the Gentile shore they were met by a man so violently possessed that shackles and chains could not contain him (Mk 5:1-20). His violence even turned on himself when he bruised himself with stones. Through the wounded body of the man the demons threw themselves at the feet of Jesus. They begged Jesus not to torment them (did the *tormenting* begin when Jesus calmed the storm?). The demons called themselves *Legion* and pleaded with Jesus to let them enter into a herd of swine feeding on a nearby hillside. When Jesus allowed this, the possessed herd of swine rushed down the hill and drowned in the sea.

Let us pause a moment here and consider the spectacle of the swine from the swineherds' point of view. You are out herding your swine (clearly you are a Gentile), as you have done many a day before. You have probably become used to staying a safe distance from that frightening man who lives among the tombs. But today something curious happens: a boatful of Jews lands ashore dangerously close to the crazed man's haunts. And lo, here comes the possessed man now, falling on the ground before one of them. There seems to be some kind of discussion, but being at a distance you can't hear or even imagine what it could be. Next thing you know, all of your swine (about 2,000) run down the hill and drown themselves. You probably don't stick around long enough to notice that the crazy man now seems to be perfectly fine.

The swineherds ran into town to report what had happened. The townspeople came out to see for themselves; and the floating swine carcasses verified the report, as did the formerly possessed man, who was now in his right mind. Understandably shocked by this bizarre and confusing scene, the people begged Jesus and his friends to leave their district.

Notice what the demons have done: they have made the townspeople frightened of Jesus, sort of like how the Jews were frightened by God when he presented himself on the mountain through fire and brimstone (Ex 20:18-19, see p. 58-60). The townspeople might have been suspicious of these Jewish men anyway, but 2,000 dead pigs certainly didn't help. Jesus immediately obliged and got back into the boat, just as his father obliged the Jews and did not continue to be present to them through a strange and frightening spectacle.

As Jesus and his disciples were getting into the boat to leave, the healed man pleaded with Jesus to let him to remain with him. Not only had no one been able to heal this man, but it seems that people had given up on him. Jesus, instead, loved him. He loved the violence out of him. If it is understandable that the townspeople want Jesus to leave, it is even more understandable that this man wants to stay with Jesus.

Jesus, however, does not permit him. This seems strange. Isn't Jesus the one who says, *Follow me*? Perhaps Jesus knows that if he returns to the Jewish shore with a Gentile in his company he will cause unnecessary scandal to Jews who may otherwise be open to him. But, more importantly, Jesus tells the healed man to stay in Gentile territory and announce to his family what has happened to him.

After some time passes, Jesus and his disciples return to the Gentile side. This time, when he arrives the people bring a deaf man to him, whom he heals (Mk 7:31-37). At some point the crowd becomes so large that Jesus pities them; and just as Jesus first multiplied loaves and fishes in Jewish territory, he now does the same for about 4,000 Gentiles (Mk 8:1-10). What happened between his first landing in that district and this return trip?

Perhaps it was that one healed Gentile man who showed himself to his family. The people were frightened of the Jewish man who seemingly caused the pigs to drown, but they were not frightened of one of their own. And the healed Gentile wouldn't have had to say much to arouse their curiosity; simply being in his right mind was witness enough. To the question, "What happened?" he would recount his story. Not from the distant point of view of the swineherds, but from his own vantage point: being gazed upon up close, and gazing back upon the face of Jesus. This gaze had penetrated to his very depths and brought an unimagined freedom and an unexpected hope.

That man's demeanor, his very presence pointed to Jesus. He was, perhaps, a greater sign of Jesus' presence in that district than Jesus himself could have been. These pagans may not have even heard of a Messiah. If they did, they might have heard he was coming to save the Jews; but what difference would that make to them? Jesus was alien to them. This healed Gentile was not.

Because the Jews backed up in fright from

God's majestic presence on the mountain, God promised to send them a prophet from among their own. When the Gentiles of that district begged Jesus to leave, he did just that; but not before providing them with the healed man, a prophet of his presence.

As Jesus began his mission to the Samaritans in Sychar with one woman, he inaugurated a mission to the Gentiles with this one man.

Through the flesh of that man, we can say that Jesus took flesh among those Gentiles: a prophecy of how he would continue to take flesh through the members of his Church, in whatever age, from whatever place, and whatever ethnicity they might be.

"Land of Zebulun and land of Naphtali,
the way to the sea, beyond the Jordan,
Galilee of the Gentiles,
the people who sit in darkness
have seen a great light,
on those dwelling in a land overshadowed by death
light has arisen."
(Mt 4:15-16, cf. Is 9:1-2)

CHAPTER 6

◦·ᴥ◦⁄⁊ʘ⁊⁄◦ᴥ·◦

He Is Risen in the Flesh

Incarnation, Resurrection, and the Two Marys

The Incarnation and the Resurrection are inextricably linked. Jesus' Death and Resurrection could not happen without the Incarnation; yet without the Resurrection of Jesus in the flesh, the Incarnation would be locked in time, a beautiful but distant memory.

In his providence, God designated two Marys to be the first witnesses of each of these events. Mary, the sinless Virgin, receives the announcement of the Incarnation from the Angel Gabriel. Mary Magdalene, from whom seven demons had been cast out (Lk 8:2), was the first witness of the Resurrected body of Christ. In Jewish tradition, seven implies completion, for God rested on the seventh day (Gn 2:2). Thus, to say that Mary Magdalene had been bound by seven demons is to say that she seemed completely lost to evil, completely without hope.

117

Mary, conceived without sin, and Mary, who had been completely bound by sin, are sister witnesses to these sister events.

The Mother of Jesus witnesses to the trustful and hopeful Yes that brings Christ into our lives. The Magdalene assures us that no amount of darkness can hold back the light of his resurrection, if our hearts yearn and beg for his mercy.

In the Risen Jesus' appearance to his Apostles in the Upper Room we see the essential unity between Incarnation and Resurrection.

The Appearances in the Upper Room

When the Apostles first saw the Risen Jesus they backed away in fright. Why? Because they thought they were seeing a ghost. How did Jesus vanquish their fear so that they might approach him? He assured them that he was with them in the flesh. *Touch me and see, because a ghost does not have flesh and bones as you can see I have* (Lk 24:39). When they saw that he was with them in the flesh, the Apostles' terror turned to joy. He continued to emphasize that he was Risen in the flesh by showing them the wounds of his crucifixion. He insisted they give him something to eat, and he ate a fish in front of them.

When Thomas, who was not there for the first appearance, refused to believe, the Risen Jesus appeared again and invited Thomas to touch his hands and to put his own hand into the wound in his side.

But those appearances in the Upper Room were not the only appearances. There were others in which the Risen Jesus was in the flesh, but the flesh was not immediately recognized to be the Risen Jesus. As it took Jacob time to realize that the man who wrestled with him was God, there were Resurrection appearances in which it took disciples time to realize that the seemingly ordinary man they were encountering was Jesus, truly Risen.

The Appearance to Mary Magdalene

After reporting to Peter and John that the tomb was empty, Mary Magdalene apparently followed behind them after they ran to see for themselves. While John's Gospel indicates that Mary Magdalene was the first witness of the Resurrected Jesus in the flesh, it seems that John, the beloved disciple, was the first to believe in the Resurrection.

Perhaps Peter and John shared Mary's assumption that the body had been taken from the tomb, but when John walked into the tomb (after respectfully allowing Peter to go in first) he saw the burial cloths there. Why would you strip a body of the burial cloths before stealing it? But what seems to have convinced John more was the head covering, not with the rest of the burial cloths but rolled up in a separate place. The beloved disciple saw these things and he believed. John's Gospel emphasizes that the disciple did not believe because he understood the Scripture that Jesus had to rise from the dead, but because of what he saw in front of him. Was that head covering rolled up in the way that the disciple saw Jesus roll up his bedclothes as they traveled from place to place?

After they inspected the empty tomb, Peter and John returned home, but Mary stayed, and wept. When she peered inside the tomb she saw two angels, who asked her why she was weeping. Still assuming the body had been taken, she replied, *They have taken my Lord, and I don't know where they laid him* (Jn 20:13). Then she turned around and saw a man standing there who asked her whom she was looking for.

Mary assumed that this man was the gardener. Let us stop and consider how different this Resurrection appearance is from those in the Upper Room. This man must not have had wounds in his hands, or she would have noticed them. He did not have a halo or a radiant light shining around him. He must have looked pretty ordinary, because she thought he was a gardener. Just some man. She wondered if he was the man who took the body and demanded, *Tell me where you laid him, and I will take him* (Jn 20:15). This, by the way, is a beautiful expression of her love for Jesus. Peter and John had left; she was alone. How did she intend to carry a dead body by herself? Her love for Jesus did not hesitate before obstacles.

Perhaps it is because Jesus was moved by this expression of her love that he exclaimed her name, *Mary!*

As soon as she heard him say her name, she realized that this was not just some man; this was Jesus. She didn't recognize him from how he looked; he didn't look like himself. She recognized him by what he did. He spoke her name with that exhortative tenderness so characteristic of Jesus.

The Appearance to the Disciples on the Road to Emmaus

The same day the empty tomb was discovered, two disciples were leaving Jerusalem for a village called Emmaus. While on their way, they encountered some man along the road. At the outset, the only thing they found exceptional about the man was that he seemed unaware of what had just happened in Jerusalem. They explained to him that Jesus was a prophet who had been handed over to death. They told about the reports of his tomb being empty, but this news did not change their downcast demeanor. The man then told them that they were foolish and slow to believe.

He then recounted to them the Hebrew Scriptures that indicate that the Messiah would have to suffer in order to enter into his glory. They were so taken by the authority with which he spoke of Scripture that they when they came near to the village and he seemed to be going on farther, they asked him to stay with them.

While he was with them at table, he took bread, said the blessing, broke it, and gave it to them. With that, their eyes were opened and they recognized him, but he vanished from their sight (Lk 24:30-31).

They recognized him in the breaking of the bread. This passage speaks to the continued presence of Christ in the Eucharist; he vanished from their sight as a man at table with them, but was still just as truly present with them through the Eucharist that he had confected. In fact, the entire encounter has the form of a liturgy; the Eucharist was preceded by his explanation of Scripture.

The two disciples admit that they should have known it was Jesus even before they recognized him in the breaking of the bread: *Were not out hearts burning [within us] while he spoke to us on the way and opened the scriptures to us?* (Lk 24:32). Their hearts were burning as they would burn when Jesus spoke to them. When that man spoke with the certainty so characteristic of Jesus, they should have recognized that he was not some man, but Jesus, alive, in the flesh.

Like Mary Magdalene, they did not recognize the man on the road by his physical appearance, but by what he did: the way he blessed and broke the bread, the way he opened the Scriptures.

The Appearance at the Sea of Tiberias

Peter decided to go fishing and some of the disciples joined him, including James and John. It was a bad night for fishing, and at dawn some man on the shore called to them and asked if they caught anything, probably an annoying question when you have to answer "No." The man told them to cast their net to the right side of the boat for a catch. When they followed his advice they came up with so many fish they couldn't pull the net in. This is reminiscent of one of Peter's early encounters with

Jesus, when Jesus preached from Peter's boat after a bad night of fishing, and Jesus had them lower the nets to make a great catch of fish (Lk 5:1-11).

The first to make the connection and recognize the man on the shore to be Jesus was the beloved disciple, who immediately told Peter, *It is the Lord* (Jn 21:7). John, who was so merciful and respectful toward Peter as to allow him to enter the empty tomb first, again showed tender consideration for his friend.

Peter swam ashore and got to Jesus first. When the others arrived they saw that Jesus had been cooking breakfast for them. And then John's Gospel makes a very curious observation: *None of the disciples dared to ask him, "Who are you?" because they realized it was the Lord* (Jn 21:12).

John was the first to realize the man was Jesus, but the others quickly made the same conclusion. But at no point during this appearance did that man physically look like Jesus. If he had, they would have had no urge to ask him "Who are you?" They were tempted to ask, but did not dare. Their certainty that he was

Jesus, not by his physical appearance but by his actions, was strong enough that they knew that to ask "Who are you?" would have been inappropriate, even unfaithful.

Why?

The apostles were tempted to ask, "Who?" For us, the pressing question is "Why?"

Why would the Risen Jesus choose at least three times to appear in a way that he was not physically recognizable? Why did he come to them not looking like himself? The Resurrection is an extremely important event. These appearances are among the most climactic and revelatory moments in salvation history.

Jesus certainly didn't intend to shroud his Resurrection in ambiguity. Consider how clear and concrete he was when he showed himself in the Upper Room. So why in these three appearances does he have the bearing of some ordinary person?

I wonder if he did this not so much for the benefit of Mary Magdalene and the disciples going to Emmaus and Peter and the fishermen, but rather for us—for us Christians who would came to believe in him in the ensuing years, decades, and centuries. We know we were on Jesus' mind at that time, because he spoke of us to Thomas, *Have you come to believe because you have seen me? Blessed are those who have not seen and have believed?* (Jn 20:29).

How could this have been for us? Because the way that 99.99% of Jesus' disciples encounter him is not through the physical face of Jesus of Nazareth, but through the face of an ordinary man or woman. We recognize Christ in them not because of their physical features but because of the way they live, because of the life of Christ that lives in them and reveals itself through them.

Saint Teresa of Calcutta did not look like Jesus of Nazareth, but was she not his fascinating and attractive presence for so many? Likewise, Saint John Paul II, Saint Josephine Bakhita, Saint Paul Miki, and every saint in every age. Likewise those saints who are not canonized, and those witnesses in our lives who have been the presence of Christ for us.

The Samaritan woman was somehow the face of Christ in that village, as was the healed Gentile among the Gentiles. They were foreshadowings of his even more real and sacramental presence in the baptized, who would become members of the Risen and Mystical Body of Christ which is the Church, and thus continue the Incarnation of Christ though the ages.

As Jesus foreshadowed this mode of continued presence through his Church by sending the Apostles and the Samaritan woman and the Gentile, so it seems he is making the same proclamation through the prophetic act of appearing as some man in the garden, along the road, and on the shore. In all three cases, the physical dissimilarity did not mask the presence of the Risen Christ. A presence that was not far away, but right there with them. God with us, in the flesh.

"I will not believe"

This can help us understand the correction to Thomas. We might think of Thomas as the unfortunate Apostle who missed that first Resurrection appearance. But perhaps Thomas was preferred. Perhaps he was chosen to be the forerunner of all of us who will come to know Christ through those whose lives are changed by him.

Ten of the Apostles, ten of Thomas' friends proclaimed to him, *We have seen the Lord* (Jn 20:25). But their witness was not just their words. The Apostles must have been moved, vibrating, radiating joy in a way they never had before. In his refusal to believe, Thomas is not only rejecting their words; he is doubting the very life that emanates from them. He is refusing to trust the new life visible in his friends, whose exclamation is an invitation to him to share their joy. The townspeople followed the Samaritan woman and believed because of her. Faced with an even greater transformation in his closest friends, Thomas refuses to believe.

Perhaps Jesus corrects him because he has rejected the method by which Jesus' subsequent disciples would come to believe. He failed to be the forerunner of all of us whose faith has come through some man or some woman.

Do not be unbelieving, but believe (Jn 20:27).

"We were hoping"

Why is it necessary that the Incarnation and Resurrection perdure in every place and every age? Why must Jesus prophesy and provide this way to continue to walk closely with us in the flesh? The disciples on the road to Emmaus can help us understand.

Recall that when they recounted to the man on the road what happened in Jerusalem, they told him that Jesus *was a prophet mighty in deed and word* (Lk 24:19). But after the crucifixion all they could say was, *We were hoping that he would be the one to redeem Israel* (Lk 24:21).

They *were hoping*, but not anymore. The mighty words and deeds no longer mean much when they are in the past. They might be a nice memory. They might give you some stories to tell your grandchildren, or even inspire some poetry and song, but they are not something that can really sustain your hope. They hold no promise for your real life, which is lived in the present.

As those disciples were remembering Jesus nostalgically, thinking of him as no longer in this world, he was right there before them, accompanying them on the very road they were walking. But his proximity did not have an impact until they became aware that he was there, until they recognized him in the flesh. That is what sent them running back to Jerusalem—or, rather, running forward.

Jesus made a promise to us, *I am with you always* (Mt 28:20). Jesus is God made flesh, so if he is with us, he must remain in the flesh. This promise is not an extra added benefit; it is essential to Christianity if our faith and hope are to remain alive and real. Because as soon as we conceive of Jesus as absent or far away, our hope withers.

The disciples on the road to Emmaus witness to the impotence of a notion of Jesus as an admired ghost of the past. Those same disciples witness to us the hope and new life that come from recognizing Christ as alive and present, and with us always.

Touch me and see, because a ghost does not have flesh and bones as you can see I have. (Lk 24:39)

Then some man wrestled with him until the break of dawn…. Jacob said, "I will not let you go until you bless me."… Jacob named the place Peniel, "Because I have seen God face to face." (Gen 32:25, 27, 31)

PART III

CHRIST PRESENT TO
THE WORLD THROUGH
THE CHURCH

Chapter 7

❧❧❧❧❧❧

Pentecost:
Through the Spirit He becomes Flesh

Ascension and Pentecost Foreshadowed

During the period of the kings, God raised up prophets. Kings ascended the throne through familial succession, but prophets were chosen directly by God, as the judges had been before the people asked for a human king. The people's rejection of God as their king did not stop God from staying close to them through his chosen prophets.

Of these, perhaps the most renowned is Elijah, who performed great signs, not the least of which was raising a boy from the dead (1 Kgs 17:17-24). Elijah called Elisha to be his attendant, and Elisha followed him faithfully. So faithfully, in fact, that on the day that Elijah was to be taken up to heaven he told Elisha to stop following him and allow him to go on alone to Bethel, and then to Jericho and then to Jordan. Elisha repeatedly asserted, *I will not leave you* (2 Kgs 2:2, 4, 6).

As a young priest, I was taking the parish youth group into Manhattan for a theatre trip, and the other adult chaperone cancelled at the last minute. I expressed to my pastor that I was concerned about losing track of the kids as we went on and off subways and walked around the city. He told me not to worry, that the students would be watching me more than I was watching them, because most of them did not go to the city too often and they themselves would not want to get lost. Likewise, Elisha had no intention of losing Elijah and the experience of God that he had brought into his life, and to the life of Israel. Where Elijah went, Elisha would go.

So they came to the Jordan, and Elijah used his cloak to part the water so he could cross over, and Elisha followed him right through. Elijah turned to Elisha and said, *Ask for whatever I may do for you, before I am taken from you* (2 Kgs 2:9). And Elisha asked Elijah for a double portion of his spirit.

What does this insightful request imply? Elisha knows how important Elijah's presence has been for Israel, and for him. If the divine presence that Elijah bore becomes a memento of the past, no amount of recollections and anecdotes that Elisha recounts will make a difference. Israel needs Elijah's spirit to remain with them. Elijah recognizes that Elisha has asked for something great, and tells him that if he sees Elijah as he is taken up, his request will be granted.

As the fiery chariot comes and lifts Elijah away, Elisha cries out, *My father! my father!* (2 Kgs 2:12). He immediately laments Elijah's absence as he watches the prophet ascend until he can see him no longer. He picks up Elijah's cloak, which had fallen from him, and he journeys home. When he comes to the Jordan he cries, *Where is the LORD, the God of Elijah?* (2 Kgs 2:14). Thanks to Elijah, God was no longer abstract for Elisha. He had become so accustomed to God's presence through Elijah that he does not identify the Lord as *the God of Abraham, Isaac, and Jacob*, but as *the God of Elijah*.

As the cry arises from the depths of his being, he slams the water of the Jordan…and it parts. Where is the God of Elijah? He is with Elisha.

Elisha realizes that Elijah's spirit has come to rest on him. In fact, fifty guild prophets went in search of Elijah even though Elisha advised against it. When they returned after three days without finding Elijah, Elisha said, *Did I not tell you not to go?* (2 Kgs 2:18). They needn't have searched for Elijah, because he was not lost.

Elijah had indeed been taken up to the Lord, but he was not absent from Israel. The fruits of Elijah's prophecy and ministry would continue to nourish God's chosen people through the flesh and blood of Elisha, who had received and was now enlivened by the spirit of Elijah. Elisha would go on to become a great prophet like Elijah. He, too, would raise a boy from the dead and perform many other signs and healings. He would cone to be held in awed reverence by Israel, as his "father" Elijah had been.

Elisha and the fifty prophets initially looked upon Elijah's being taken up as a lamentable loss. But when Elisha's actions made it clear that Elijah's spirit remained in him, and thus remained with Israel, they recognized God's faithfulness and generosity to be greater than they had imagined. Elijah's being taken up was the precursor to a promise being fulfilled.

Similarly and mysteriously, the Ascension of Jesus would not be a loss to the Apostles, but rather the prelude to the promised coming of the Spirit, and thus the beginning of the Church, i.e., the Mystical Body of Christ enlivened by the Holy Spirit and witnessing to the world that Christ remains with us.

Ascension and Pentecost Fulfilled

The Gospel of John recounts that, during the Last Supper discourses, Jesus promised to send the Holy Spirit. Luke reveals that Jesus continued to speak of the coming of the Holy Spirit even after his Resurrection. *While meeting with them, he enjoined them not to depart from Jerusalem, but to wait for "the promise of the Father about which you have heard me speak; for John baptized with water, but in a few days you will be baptized with the holy Spirit"* (Acts 1:4-5).

Just before he ascended to the Father, Jesus repeated this promise: *You will receive power when the holy Spirit comes upon you, and you will be my witnesses in Jerusalem, throughout Judea and Samaria, and to the ends of the earth* (Acts 1:8).

As Jesus is taken up from them, the Apostles look up intently at the sky, just as Elisha watched until he could see Elijah no more. As Elisha awaited the spirit promised by Elijah, the Apostles wait for the Holy Spirit, the promise of the Father through which they would become witnesses to Jesus' continued presence. While Jesus is ascending from their sight, two mysterious men stand beside the Apostles and address them, *Men of Galilee, why are you standing there looking at the sky? This Jesus who has been taken up from you into heaven will return in the same way as you have seen him going into heaven* (Acts 1:11). As he ascends now, so he will descend. As the Holy Spirit descended upon Mary and Jesus took flesh in her womb, so the Holy Spirit will descend upon the Apostles and Jesus will take flesh through them.

In fact, Mary was there at Pentecost (Acts 1:14). She was there when the driving wind filled the house and the Holy Spirit filled the Apostles and enabled them to proclaim Jesus to the diverse crowd that had gathered. All but one of these Apostles had been too fearful to accompany Jesus to the cross. All of these Apostles had questioned him and were tempted to resist him when he made it clear that he would be handed over in Jerusalem. But when the Holy Spirit came upon them, they preached without fear. They proclaimed Jesus with the same authority with which Jesus had proclaimed the Father. As Jesus not only spoke about the Father but bore his very presence (*Whoever has seen me has seen the Father* [Jn 14:9]), so the Apostles, filled with the Holy Spirit, bore in their words and in their very persons the presence of Christ.

It is important to note that the presence of Christ manifested through the Apostles is not generic. *Then there appeared to them tongues as of fire, which parted and came to rest on each one of them* (Acts 2:3). A flame came to rest on *each one.* Christ's presence is brought forth in a unique and personal way through each person who receives the Spirit.

What must Pentecost have been like for Mary? She who was the first to be overshadowed by the Holy Spirit, who accepted her Yes and made Jesus present in her. She had become the Mother of God, and at the cross her Son called her to become the Mother of his beloved disciple. She must have pondered the meaning of that in her heart; and perhaps on Pentecost, after waiting for the Spirit with the Apostles, her pondering received a response. She saw all of the Apostles witnessing in a new way. That was John, but he had the life, the energy, the spirit of her Son. It was still Peter, but she recognized in him the living authority of Jesus.

As we are sometimes amazed when we suddenly recognize the mannerisms of our parents or grandparents in our children or nephews and nieces, how much more profoundly must Mary have recognized her Risen Son in each of the Apostles, and begun to understand what it meant that she was the Mother of the Church. For the one born from her womb was being born again in the world through the flesh of the Apostles. They would be the foundations of his Church, which would not be a merely human organization, but a sacrament of his Person, alive and present in the world. The Mother of the Son of God, human and divine, was now the Mother of the Church, human and divine. The Incarnation was not only an event of the past; it was happening in the present. Jesus would dwell among us through the Church, and the Acts of the Apostles clearly traces the life of Christ lived in his Mystical Body.

The Descent of the Spirit upon Jesus, the Descent of the Spirit upon the Apostles

Jesus did not publicly preach or perform a miracle or a healing until the day of his baptism, when the Holy Spirit descended upon him and the voice of the Father affirmed, *You are my beloved Son; with you I am well pleased* (Mk 1:11). All that Jesus did was an expression of his belonging to the Father, an overflowing of the love the Father gave and that Jesus welcomed and returned. Saint Augustine teaches us that the Holy Spirit is the love between the Father and the Son.[6] The Father's love overflowed through Jesus like a fount of living water and brought life to all who welcomed him. The Father is at the core of Jesus' authority, his words, his deeds, and his love. Jesus' identity is that of the beloved Son. This is so true that when the devil tries to tempt Jesus, the first phrase of the temptations is *if you are the Son of God* (Mt 4:3). The devil tries to place doubt in the relationship which is the essence of who Jesus is. If you recall, the original sin occurred after the devil placed doubt in the relationship between our first parents and God. They thought reality could have substance without God. Jesus, when offered all the kingdoms of the world, knows the devil's promise is empty because reality has no meaning without God. Without love, which originates from the Father, all of reality, every word and deed, is a meaningless and clanging cymbal (1 Cor 13:1).

This is why Jesus tells the disciples to wait in Jerusalem until they are baptized with the Holy Spirit (Acts 1:4-5). He does not want them to preach or heal until they are generated by his presence in the Spirit, as he is always generated by the Father in the unity of the Holy Spirit. Recall that Jesus told his Apostles, *without me you can do nothing* (Jn 15:5). The teaching of the Apostles would be fruitless without the Spirit. They would just be men recounting facts of the past. Elisha knew that Israel needed the presence of Elijah, not merely stories about what he did. The world needs the living presence of Christ; words are not enough. When the Spirit comes upon the Apostles at Pentecost, Jesus is with them and within them even more than he was before. All of the words and deeds of the Apostles will flow from the presence of Christ, who generates them with the love of the Father.

As Jesus' public ministry begins only after the Spirit descends and the Father affirms his love, so the ministry of the Church begins only after the descent of the Holy Spirit at Pentecost, making Jesus incarnate in the Church.

The Ministry of Jesus, the Ministry of Peter

On the day of Pentecost itself, Peter, who had betrayed Jesus out of fear, stood up with the rest of the Eleven and preached to the people with the same authority as Jesus. His fearless authority comes through the Spirit who has filled him, and who also encourages him through the other Apostles, who are with him. About 3,000 people were so moved by Peter's preaching and by the Apostles that they became disciples, not unlike the thousands who followed Jesus, for whom he multiplied loaves.

Not long after Pentecost, Peter healed a man who had been crippled from birth. *When he saw Peter and John about to go into the temple, he asked for alms. But Peter looked intently at him, as did John, and said, "Look at us." He paid attention to them, expecting to receive something from them. Peter said, "I have neither silver nor gold, but what I do have I give you: in the name of Jesus Christ the Nazorean, [rise and] walk." Then Peter took him by the right hand and raised him up, and immediately his feet and ankles grew strong.... When all the people saw him walking and praising God, they recognized him as the one who used to sit begging at the Beautiful Gate of the temple, and they were filled with amazement and astonishment at what had happened to him* (Acts 3:3-10). Is this Peter? Yes, it is Peter, filled with the Holy Spirit; it is Peter, who has become another Christ.

Later, Luke tells us that *they even carried the sick out into the streets and laid them on cots and mats so that when Peter came by, at least his shadow might fall on one or another of them* (Acts 5:15). They are bringing the sick to a fisherman from Galilee; they are seeking healing from the shadow of a sinner. Later on, Peter will raise a woman named Tabitha from death (Acts 9:36-43). Peter has become the presence of Christ. And it is not only Peter; Luke tells that all of the Apostles did signs and wonders among the people (Acts 5:12).

Jesus' public ministry continues through the Apostles, because Jesus himself is ministering through the Apostles.

The Arrest of Jesus, the Arrest of Peter and John
Very early in Jesus' ministry, the religious authorities opposed him. After the first healing that Peter performs in the name of Jesus, the

religious authorities came to confront him and arrest him along with John, who was with him.

The next day Peter and John were brought before the high priest and the Sanhedrin. This is the same Sanhedrin that had Jesus arrested and interrogated. The fear of being brought before this assembly may have been the reason that Peter had denied Jesus.

Now, that same Peter, filled with the Holy Spirit, answers the Sanhedrin's interrogation directly and strongly: *If we are being examined today about a good deed done to a cripple, namely, by what means he was saved, then all of you and all the people of Israel should know that it was in the name of Jesus Christ the Nazorean whom you crucified, whom God raised from the dead; in his name this man stands before you healed. He is "the stone rejected by you, the builders, which has become the cornerstone." There is no salvation through anyone else, nor is there any other name under heaven given to the human race by which we are to be saved"* (Acts 4:9-12).

The Sanhedrin thought they had solved the problem of Jesus. But before they condemned him they must have been surprised by the authority of the Galilean carpenter who would not be bullied by their power. They had never seen anything like it. Until this day, when two Galilean fishermen were just as unshakable before their show of power. The religious authority the Sanhedrin tries to wield so threateningly pales before the authority of Peter and John, and they cannot help but notice. *Observing the boldness of Peter and John and perceiving them to be uneducated, ordinary men, they were amazed, and they recognized them as the companions of Jesus* (Acts 4:13).

They thought they had taken care of Jesus, and now there were two more of him standing before them. And note the way in which they recognized Peter and John to be Jesus' companions. It was not because they remembered their faces as men who had followed Jesus. Nor that they had recognized their accents, as happened to Peter on the night of Jesus' trial. They recognize them as companions of Jesus because of their boldness.

Recall that even those who were not followers of Jesus, like Pilate or the rich young man, could recognize his exceptionality. The Sanhedrin, who had handed Jesus over to Pilate, could not deny his exceptionality. And that same exceptionality was before them again, living in Peter and John, suffering persecution in and with Peter and John. The Sanhedrin recognized them not by their physical looks, but by their impossibly authoritative demeanor. The angel Gabriel had promised Mary, *nothing will be impossible for God* (Lk 1:37).

The Death of Jesus, the Death of Stephen

Stephen was one of the deacons that were chosen and brought before the Apostles to have their hands laid on them. He was *a man filled with faith and the holy Spirit* (Acts 6:5). Stephen, like the Apostles, was working great signs among the people, and, like Peter and John, he quickly ran into opposition. His opponents *could not withstand the wisdom and the spirit with which he spoke* (Acts 6:10), and so they brought false accusations against him and brought him before the Sanhedrin, just as had been done to Jesus.

He, too, spoke without fear before the Sanhedrin. Those who heard him were so incensed by his boldness that they threw him out of the city and began to stone him. Recall that Jesus was crucified outside of the city (Jn 19:20; Heb 13:12). Stephen suffers his martyrdom in a way remarkably similar to the way Jesus suffered his crucifixion.

> *Then Jesus said, "Father forgive them, they know not what they do."* (Lk 23:34)

> *[Stephen] fell to his knees and cried out in a loud voice, "Lord, do not hold this sin against them."* (Acts 7:60)

> *Jesus cried out in a loud voice, "Father, into your hands I commend my spirit."* (Lk 23:46)

> *As they were stoning Stephen, he called out, "Lord Jesus, receive my spirit."* (Acts 7:59)

Recall the Roman soldier who was so amazed when he saw the way Jesus died, and declared,

Truly this man was the Son of God (Mk 15:39). Stephen died praying to the Lord and begging forgiveness for his persecutors, just as Jesus did. He was filled with the Holy Spirit as they led him away to his death, an ordinary man dying in an extraordinary way, because his Lord was living in him even as he was dying.

The Risen Jesus on the Road, Philip on the Road

Stephen's martyrdom was the beginning of a persecution of the Church in Jerusalem that caused many disciples to scatter throughout Judea and Samaria, including Philip, one of the deacons originally chosen with Stephen. Sometime after he preached in the city of Samaria, *the angel of the Lord spoke to Philip, "Get up and head south on the road that goes down from Jerusalem to Gaza* (Acts 8:26). An Ethiopian eunuch who had gone to Jerusalem to worship was returning home on that road.

> *The Spirit said to Philip, "Go and join up with that chariot." Philip ran up and heard him reading Isaiah the prophet and said, "Do you understand what you are reading?"*

He replied, "How can I, unless someone
instructs me?" So he invited Philip to get
in and sit with him. This was the scripture
passage he was reading:

> *"Like a sheep he was led to the slaughter,*
> *and as a lamb before its shearer is silent,*
> *so he opened not his mouth.*
> *In [his] humiliation justice was denied*
> *him.*
> *Who will tell of his posterity?*
> *For his life is taken from the earth."*

(Acts 8:29-33)

The Ethiopian is reading from Isaiah 53, which refers to a man who will suffer and die for the people. He cannot understand what the Scripture means, and recognizes that the written words are not enough; he needs a person to instruct him. In explaining the passage to him, Philip proclaims Jesus. His proclamation is so convincing that when they pass by a body of water the Ethiopian has the chariot stopped and asks Philip to baptize him.

After Philip baptized the Ethiopian, *the Spirit of the Lord snatched Philip away, and the eunuch saw him no more, but continued on his way rejoicing* (Acts 8:39).

Does this seem familiar? It is like a scene-by-scene reenactment of the Risen Jesus walking on the road away from Jerusalem with the disciples who were on their way to Emmaus. Jesus recounted to those disciples the Scriptures that referred to the suffering Messiah. Those Scriptures almost surely included Isaiah 53, which Philip explained in the chariot. In both cases, after Scripture is cited and explained a sacrament is celebrated. On the way to Emmaus it was the Eucharist. On the road toward Gaza it is baptism. After the sacrament was confected, Jesus, and later Philip, acting in the person of Jesus, disappeared from sight.

Both scenes resemble a liturgy, and in each encounter the disappearance does not cause disappointment, because the presence of Christ remains. The Ethiopian goes on his way rejoicing, because just as Christ was so obviously present through Philip, he now remains present with the eunuch through his baptism. The inspired words that the Ethiopian was reading were fulfilled in the Word made flesh: first in the Incarnation of Christ, and then sacramentally in Philip, and then in the Ethiopian himself.

The Church so truly continues the presence of Christ that the earthly life of Jesus is relived in the Church's earliest members. The baptism of the Lord re-occurs when the Apostles are baptized with the Holy Spirit. The public ministry of Jesus lives on in the ministry of Peter and the Apostles. The arrest of Jesus is seen again in the arrest of Peter and John. The exceptional way that Stephen dies is a clear echo of the way that Jesus died. Philip on the road is a step-by-step continuation of the road that Jesus took with two disciples in need of his presence.

Through the Church Jesus is really and tangibly with us. We all have reason, like the Ethiopian, to continue on our way rejoicing. For he accompanies us along our way.

The Mission to Jews, Samaritans, and Gentiles
Do not go into pagan territory or enter a Samaritan town. Go rather to the lost sheep of the house of Israel. (Mt 10:5-6)

You will receive power when the holy Spirit comes upon you, and you will my witnesses in Jerusalem, throughout Judea and Samaria, and to the ends of the earth. (Acts 1:8)

The Church even follows the same missionary path as Jesus. As Jesus went first to Jews, and then to Samaritans and Gentiles, the Acts of the Apostles shows that the early disciples do the same.

At Pentecost the Apostles are preaching to Jews who had come to Jerusalem to worship.

When the deacon Philip leaves Jerusalem after Stephen's martyrdom, he goes to the city of Samaria and proclaims Jesus, while performing signs and curing the sick. When the Apostles heard that the Samaritans had received Philip and thus accepted Jesus, they sent Peter and John to them to pray with them and lay hands on them, that they might receive the Holy Spirit.

The mission to the Gentiles is seen in Philip instructing and baptizing the Ethiopian, and later when Peter teaches and baptizes Cornelius:

The circumcised believers who had accompanied Peter were astounded that the gift of the holy Spirit should have been poured out on the Gentiles also (Acts 10:45).

Even more Gentiles would come to encounter and believe in Jesus through the missionary vocation of Paul.

Chapter 8

⁓೦ଔଔ೦⁓

Paul, Apostle of the Mystical Body of Christ

Paul's Conversion and
the Church as Christ Himself

The identity of Jesus with his Church is strikingly expressed in his dialogue with Saul. Saul had approved of the killing of Stephen, and he was going to Damascus to arrest more Christians, who at that point were called followers of *the Way*. Saul's own way to Damascus was interrupted by Jesus himself.

> *On his journey, as he was nearing Damascus, a light from the sky suddenly flashed around him. He fell to the ground and heard a voice saying to him, "Saul, Saul, why are you persecuting me?" He said, "Who are you, sir?" The reply came, "I am Jesus, whom you are persecuting"* (Acts 9:3-5).

Jesus refers to his followers as *me*. Not "them," but "me." And if that's not clear enough, when Saul asks who is speaking to him, the answer is, *I am Jesus, whom you are persecuting.* By the time Saul comes on the scene persecuting Christians, Jesus has already died, risen, and ascended to the Father. It would thus seem that Saul had never met Jesus himself. But Jesus claims that this is not so: Saul met Jesus in each and every Christian he persecuted.

Were each of those Christians truly the presence of Jesus in the flesh? As hard as it might be to answer yes to that question, it would seem just as hard to answer no, when we consider Jesus' own words to Saul.

It was shocking when Jesus explicitly identified himself with the Eucharist, when he said, *I am the bread of life* (Jn 6:48), and then repeatedly spoke in such literal terms as, *my flesh is true food, and my blood is true drink* (Jn 6:55).

Is it any less shocking to hear him describe his followers as *me*, and as *Jesus*? And his words of identification are repeated three times in the Acts of the Apostles. In the second account, Jesus' response to Saul's *Who are you?* is even more specific, *I am Jesus the Nazorean whom you are persecuting* (Acts 22:8). Christ is really present in the Eucharist, and his words reveal that he is truly present in the members of his Church.

To Remain with Jesus Is
to Remain with the Church

Jesus instructed Paul to go into the city and wait to be told what he must do. Paul went into the city and waited, not unlike the Apostles, who waited in the Upper Room. Jesus sent Ananias to baptize Paul. *So Ananias went and entered the house; laying his hands on him, he said, "Saul, my brother, the Lord has sent me, Jesus who appeared to you on the way by which you came, that you may regain your sight and be filled with the holy Spirit." Immediately things like scales fell from his eyes and he regained his sight. He got up and was baptized, and when he had eaten, he recovered his strength* (Acts 9:17-19). As the Apostles received the Holy Spirit after their period of waiting, Paul received the Holy Spirit through the hands of Ananias.

For Paul, to remain in relationship with the Risen Christ was to remain in relationship with the members of the Church. After Paul was baptized by Ananias, he stayed with disciples in Damascus. After three years, Acts tells us that *when he arrived in Jerusalem he tried to join the disciples* (Acts 9:26). He had gained an understanding that belonging to Christ meant belonging to the community of the Church. Barnabas befriended Paul and took him to the Apostles. Paul wrote to the Galatians that one of the reasons he went to Jerusalem was to confer with Peter. Paul was much more educated than Peter and probably all of the Apostles, and perhaps a better preacher and writer, but he understood that he must be in unity with the leaders who had been chosen by Christ to bear his authoritative presence.

Paul would not go on missionary journeys alone. Barnabas was his missionary partner at the beginning; later it would be Silas, Timothy, Titus, Luke, Priscilla, Aquila, and other companions as well. When he wrote letters he would sometimes list the names of those who were with him and send greetings on their behalf, and he would also name specific people that he wanted to greet, or he would ask for people to come and help him in his ministry. As Jesus sent his disciples out two by two, Paul perceived that a brother or sister in the Faith is a privileged way that Jesus accompanies us.

Fourteen years after first visiting Peter in Jerusalem, Paul returned because of the controversy of circumcision, which arose because some Jewish Christians were claiming that circumcision was necessary to become a Christian. Paul strongly disagreed, but, again, he understood that it was not a decision he should make himself, but needed to be faced in union with the Apostles.

Paul writes, *I presented to them the Gospel that I preach to the Gentiles—but privately to those of repute—so that I might not be running, or have run, in vain* (Gal 2:2).

If what Paul encountered on the road to Damascus had been just a new religious doctrine, then there would have been no reason for him to check with the Apostles. He was perfectly capable of understanding and preaching doctrine. However, Paul encountered a Person, the Person of Jesus Christ.

And if the Risen Jesus whom Paul encountered was present only in heaven and in isolated supernatural appearances, than Paul still would not have needed to check with the Apostles. Paul had seen the Risen Jesus himself; why did he need Peter?

It is because the Risen Jesus referred to his disciples as "me" that Paul understands that Christ does not remain distant in heaven, but is alive and continually present in the members of his body, the Church.

Paul makes sure to write to the Galatians that, *when they recognized the grace bestowed upon me, James and Cephas and John, who were reputed to be pillars, gave me and Barnabas their right hands in partnership, that we should go to the Gentiles and they to the circumcised* (Gal 2:9). This approval, this partnership, guarantees that Paul is preaching the living truth.

At one point Paul even corrects Peter and writes about it to the Church (Gal 2:11-14). He is not scandalized by Peter's weakness and he is not worried that the Galatians will be scandalized. Paul recognizes that Christ's presence abides and manifests itself even in weakness.

Treasure in Earthen Vessels

Because Jesus asked him, *Why are you persecuting me?* Paul realized that Christ is present in the members of his Church. He recognized Christ in Peter, even when he corrected him for his weakness. Having become a disciple himself, Paul also recognized the mystery of the living Christ manifested in his own weak flesh. Jesus even taught Paul the value of his weaknesses: that he not become proud, and that it be clear that the good he does comes not from himself but from the power of God. For, like Moses, who asked God that his speech impediment be removed, Paul asked Jesus to remove a particular weakness, which he experienced as a thorn in his flesh. *Three times I begged the Lord about this, that it might leave me, but he said to me, "My grace is sufficient for you, for power is made perfect in weakness." I will rather boast most gladly of my weaknesses, in order that the power of Christ may dwell with me* (2 Cor 12:8-9).

Paul's "glad boasting" belies the fact that his weakness was not something he only recognized interiorly; it was apparent to those who met him. Perhaps his evident frailty made Paul a more approachable Apostle and, paradoxically, a more powerful witness. He wrote to the Corinthians: *May I not seem as one frightening you through letters. For someone will say, "His letters are severe and forceful, but his bodily presence is weak, and his speech contemptible." Such a person must understand that what we are in word through letters when absent, that we also are in action when present.... But we will not boast beyond measure but will keep to the limits God has apportioned us, namely, to reach even to you* (2 Cor 10:9-11, 13).

He commended the Galatians for welcoming him: *you know that it was because of a physical illness that I originally preached the gospel to you, and you did not show disdain or contempt because of the trial caused you by my physical condition, but rather you received me as an angel of God, as Christ Jesus* (Gal 4:13-14). And it was appropriate that they received this weak man as if they were receiving Christ Jesus; for earlier in that same letter Paul proclaims, *I have been crucified with Christ; yet I live, no longer I, but Christ lives in me* (Gal 2:19b-20a).

Since Christ lives in Paul, it should not surprise us that the scandal of the Incarnation is magnified in him, and perhaps most especially in his human frailty. What was it about Jesus himself that so outraged the Pharisees and Sadducees? That a carpenter from Nazareth could be, not just a prophet, but the very presence of God in our midst. Mark portrays how this scandal arose when Jesus went back to his own town of Nazareth: *They said, "Where did this man get all this? What kind of wisdom has been given him? What mighty deeds are wrought by his hands! Is he not the carpenter, the son of Mary, and the brother of James and Joses and Judas and Simon? And are not his sisters here with us?" And they took offense at him* (Mk 6:2-3).

It is easy to think that if I were there, I would have believed in Jesus; but let us not discount the difficulty of accepting God with us, really with us, in ordinary human flesh. And let us be aware that we are not spared the scandal of the Incarnation; we too can hesitate at the difficulty of believing and welcoming Christ among us through ordinary and frail human beings of our present day. I wonder how many times my rejection of the vessel has kept me from the treasure? And when I think of witnesses in my life whose foibles may annoy me to the point that I congratulate myself on my patience, I tremble to think about the flaws that all those whom I encounter must look past in order to recognize a faint image of Christ in me! How merciful is God to mix himself up with us!

God was not afraid of getting his hands muddy when he created Adam, and the Son of God is not afraid of the mud when he welcomes our humanity into communion with his divinity. In his book *Why the Church?* Msgr. Luigi Giussani calls this the "human factor" of the Church, and he uses the image of gold in the mud as a metaphor for Christ's presence among the men and women that God has chosen.[7] Giussani echoes Saint Paul's image of a treasure in earthen vessels.

But we hold this treasure in earthen vessels, that the surpassing power may be of God and not from us. We are afflicted in every way, but not constrained; perplexed, but not driven to despair; persecuted, but not abandoned; struck down, but not destroyed; always carrying about in the body the dying of Jesus, so that the life of Jesus may also be manifested in our body. For we who live are constantly being given up to death for the sake of Jesus, so that the life of Jesus may be manifested in our mortal flesh. (2 Cor 4:7-11)

The Church Is the Body of Christ

Paul did not perceive the Church as a merely human institution. He experienced that it was much more than an assembly of those who agree on the same doctrines. He also recognized that what unites us is deeper than the common human ancestry that unites the Jews.

The Church is the continuation in time of the presence of the living, incarnate Jesus Christ. We belong to him not because we have the same ethnic ancestry as he, but because we have received the Holy Spirit. The Spirit who made Jesus present in Mary's womb, the Spirit who makes the bread and wine become the real Body and Blood of Christ, is the Spirit who makes us members of the body of Christ, a body whose flesh is our flesh, a body in which his Spirit dwells. The Word became flesh, and in his body, the Church, he dwells among us.

Christ, the Word Incarnate, continues to scandalize, and continues to save.

As a body is one though it has many parts, and all the parts of the body, though many, are one body, so also Christ. For in one Spirit we were all baptized into one body, whether Jews or Greeks, slaves or free persons, and we were all given to drink of one Spirit.

Now the body is not a single part, but many. If a foot should say, "Because I am not a hand I do not belong to the body," it does not for this reason belong any less to the body. Or if an ear should say, "Because I am not an eye I do not belong to the body," it does not for this reason belong any less to the body. If the whole body were an eye, where would the hearing be? If the whole body were hearing, where would the sense of smell be? But as it is, God placed the parts, each one of them, in the body as he intended. If they were all one part, where would the body be? But as it is, there are many parts, yet one body. The eye cannot say to the hand, "I do not need you," nor again the head to the feet, "I do not need you." Indeed, the parts of the body that seem to be weaker are all the more necessary, and those parts of the body that we consider less honorable we surround with greater honor, and our less presentable parts are treated with greater propriety, whereas our more presentable parts do not need this. But God has so constructed the body as to give greater honor to a part that is without it, so that there may be no division in the body, but that the parts may have the same concern for one another. If [one] part suffers, all the parts suffer with it; if one part is honored, all the parts share its joy.

Now you are Christ's body, and individually parts of it. (1 Cor 12:12-27)

Living the truth in love, we should grow in every way into him who is the head, Christ, from whom the whole body, joined and held together by every supporting ligament, with the proper functioning of each part, brings about the body's growth and builds itself up in love. (Eph 4:15-16)

Conclusion

❧❦❧

The Word Became Flesh—Forever

The Nativity and the Ascension, through the Eyes of the Angels

In *The Angels and their Mission*, Cardinal Daniélou writes, "If the mystery of the Nativity inaugurates the work of Christ, that of the Ascension completes it."[8] He goes on to explain how some Fathers of the Church depict the participation of the angels in the Ascension.

In Acts, Luke tells us about two mysterious men dressed in white garments who question the Apostles who are looking intently at the sky (Acts 1:10-11).

In John's Gospel, Jesus promises his disciple Nathanael, *Amen, amen, I say to you, you will see the sky opened and the angels of God ascending and descending on the Son of Man* (Jn 1:51). This image evokes the stairway that Jacob saw in his dream. The bottom of the stairway touched the earth and the top reached to the heavens, and the angels of God were going up and down on it (Gen 28:12).

Saint John Chrysostom comments that the angels are rising and descending around Jesus because they want to contemplate the sight of a man, in flesh and blood, entering heaven.[9] And what did the angels see, according to Chrysostom? "He rose above the angels, He passed the Cherubim, He went higher than the Seraphim, He bypassed the Thrones, He did not stop until he arrived at the very throne of God."[10]

Saints Justin, Irenaeus, Athanasius, and Gregory of Nyssa witness to a tradition that sees in Psalm 24:7-10 an image of the Ascension:

Lift up your heads, O gates;
rise up, you ancient portals,
that the king of glory may enter.
Who is this king of glory?
The LORD, a mighty warrior,
the LORD, mighty in battle.
Lift up your heads, O gates;
rise up, you ancient portals,
that the king of glory may enter.

Who is this king of glory?
    The LORD *of hosts is the king of glory.*

The image proposed by these Fathers is that the angels ascending with Jesus are telling the angels in heaven to open the gates to the King of Glory. But the angels guarding heaven's gates question them. For the ascending angels are accompanying a man of flesh and blood who bears wounds in his body. That a man, that a human nature could be approaching the very throne of God causes the angels at the gates to ask again, "Who is this?" And the ascending angels, with great rejoicing, repeat their proclamation and verify that this man is indeed the King of Glory.

Daniélou writes, "The overwhelming revelation made to the angels in the mystery of the Ascension is not that they are to adore the eternal Word—that is already the object of their liturgy—but rather that they are to adore the Word Incarnate; and that overturns all of heaven, just as the Incarnation revolutionized all of earth."[11]

The Nativity proclaims that the Word became flesh. The Ascension proclaims that the eternal Word became flesh for all eternity! We have many hymns and carols with which we rejoice with the angels at the Nativity. The Ascension, not quite as much. And so we can easily make the mistake of thinking that Jesus loved us so much that he took on our human nature for thirty-three years. No! He loves us infinitely more than we imagine, because he took on our human nature forever. At the Annunciation, when he became flesh in the womb of Mary, Jesus married himself to us forever; and Jesus knows what forever is, much more than any bridegroom before or since.

If he had only become flesh for those thirty-three years, Jesus would be trapped in time, only a historical figure. The Gospels would describe great stories and events of the past, but God would remain infinitely distant from us in the present.

I remember at the end of a high school vacation/retreat, I was riding next to another teacher on the way home, and we were commenting on all the beautiful things that had happened among the students over the past week. At one point the teacher said to me, "If we are not available to help these kids continue in the encounter and relationship with Jesus that they have experienced in these days, we have done something cruel. We have given them a glimpse of something great and have not shown them how this can be more than a glimpse, but a presence that transforms their whole lives."

God did not want to tease us with a brief taste of what it could be like to have him near us. Recall that Isaiah cried, *Oh, that you would rend the heavens and come down* (Is 63:19). The cry of the Apostles must have been "Oh, that you would stay!"

Jesus came to stay! He is not a paramour; he is the Bridegroom. The Ascension is not a lamentation of his absence; it is a feast of his presence. The promise of the Holy Spirit is his promise to be with us now and forever.

I Am with You Always

If Jesus has ascended to the throne of the Father, how can he be with us? Let us consider again what Jesus said to Nathanael, *you will see the sky opened and the angels of God ascending and descending on the Son of Man* (Jn 1:51). In evoking the angels who ascend and descend the stairway in Jacob's dream, it seems that Jesus is identifying that stairway with himself. Recall that it is one stairway, with its base firmly on the ground and its top in heaven.

Through the Holy Spirit, who is the infinite love between the Father and the Son, Jesus can be with the Father in heaven and with us here on the ground. We often use the expression "I am with you in spirit," when we cannot really be with someone at a moment when we wish we could. Infinite love desires infinitely more to be with the beloved, and the Incarnation of Jesus made sure that the loving desire of Father, Son, and Holy Spirit would be forever fulfilled. When Jesus says, "I am with you in Spirit," he really is with us. And who is Jesus? He is the Word made flesh, so if he is going to be with us he must be with us somehow in the flesh.

He is with us in the community of the Church. Recall that he promised, *Where two or three are gathered together in my name, there am I in the midst of them* (Mt 18:20). This helps us understand why families and parishes and religious communities and religious movements are so important for Christians, and why the Church tells us that we must assemble regularly to worship together.

He also promises that he is with us in those who require our love. In the parable of the sheep and the goats, the king says, *"Come, you who are blessed by my Father. Inherit the kingdom prepared for you from the foundation of the world. For I was hungry and you gave me food, I was thirsty and you gave me drink, a stranger and you welcomed me, naked and you clothed me, ill and you cared for me, in prison and you visited me."* Then the righteous will answer him and say, *"Lord, when did we see you hungry and feed you, or thirsty and give you drink? When did we see you a stranger and welcome you, or naked and clothe you? When did we see you ill or in prison, and visit you?"* And the king will say to them in reply, *"Amen, I say to you, whatever you did for one of these least brothers of mine, you did for me"* (Mt 25:34-40). How many saints and religious communities have given their lives witnessing to his presence among the poor?

He dwells among us, and also within us. We don't hear a lot from Saint Jude in the Gospels, but John the Evangelist recalls an extremely important question that Jude asked. As Jesus was giving his final discourse to the Apostles at the Last Supper, Jude grasped the great significance of what Jesus was revealing about the Father and the Holy Spirit. He asked Jesus, *Master, [then] what happened that you will reveal yourself to us and not to the world?* (Jn 14:22). He wondered why Jesus was giving this testimony to twelve men around a table and not on a mountainside to thousands, as he had done before.

Jesus answered and said to him, "Whoever loves me will keep my word, and my Father will love him, and we will come to him and make our dwelling with him" (Jn 14:23). Jesus will make his dwelling with the person who loves him. With this response, it is as if Jesus it telling Jude, "I *am* revealing myself to the world, beginning with you around this table. I will dwell with you, and you will encounter others, and as they

become my disciples I will dwell with them."
Jesus is revealing himself to the world person
by person by person. It can be a slow and ineffi-
cient method, but it is the only way.

The final words of Jesus recorded in Matthew's Gospel are: *Go, therefore, and make disciples of all nations, baptizing them in the name of
the Father, and of the Son, and of the holy Spirit,
teaching them to observe all that I have commanded you. And behold, I am with you always,
until the end of the age* (Mt 28:19-20).

Behold, he tells us, *I am with you always.*
Behold what? In context it seems that we are
to behold the one we have baptized, the one we
have taught.

I can behold with joy the person I have
baptized because Christ is now present in and
through that person. Christ has again become
present with us in the flesh because that person
has become an "other Christ."

But Jesus also commands us to teach. If a
person is baptized, they objectively belong to
the body of Christ, but they need guides to help
them experience the greatness of who they are

and what it means to belong to God, who is love. How many baptized sons and daughters of the Father live as if they are orphans? What do they need? They need to encounter a person or a community where there is awareness of what we have become in Christ Jesus, i.e., they need to encounter Christ in the flesh through the way those persons love them—those persons who do not look like Jesus physically but in whom Christ dwells and reveals himself.

When a person encounters Christ's love in the flesh, and their baptism is enlivened or perhaps they are led to baptism, behold, that person, in turn, becomes a spectacle to others; yet another witness that the Word has become flesh and dwells among us. The person becomes a witness to Christ's presence in a particular way that only he or she can be, with his or her history, temperament, strengths, frailties, faith, hope, and love.

We can see an icon of this dynamic between two people who, interestingly, never personally met. In the many letters between Saint Thérèse of Lisieux and the seminarian Maurice Bellière, Maurice changes. The love that Thérèse expressed in her letters was, for him, a real experience of the embrace of Christ. In one letter she wrote to him "Your unique treasure, is it not Jesus?" (7/26/1897)[12] and he responded, "There is no doubt that Jesus is the treasure, but I found him in you. And he was easier to approach" (8/5/1897).[13] Maurice encountered Jesus' love for him incarnated in the love of Thérèse. Previous to this friendship, Maurice conceived of Jesus as distant and harsh. He imagined Jesus being disappointed with him much more often than he dared to think that Jesus might love him.

Maurice was like the Israelites at the foot of the mountain backing away from the frightening visage of God. Maurice knew intellectually that God had become flesh in Jesus; surely he had studied it in the seminary. But he did not have an experience of the Incarnation in his own life. Through Thérèse, Jesus came to Maurice in such a way that he did not back away. The Good News is not theoretical; it is the real experience of Christ that Maurice had thanks to Thérèse, and thanks to Jesus' promise to be with us always.

The essence of Christianity is Christ incarnate; and he remains among us in his Church. As he approaches us through the members of his body, he in turn becomes easier for us to approach.

In a letter he sent to Msgr. Giussani, Saint John Paul II wrote, "The road, as you have affirmed so many times, is Christ. He is the Way, the Truth, and the Life, who reaches the person in his day-to-day existence. The discovery of this road normally comes about through the mediation of other human beings. Marked through the gift of faith by the encounter with the Redeemer, believers are called to become an echo of the event of Christ, to become themselves an 'event.' Christianity, even before being a sum of doctrines or a rule for salvation, is thus the 'event' of an encounter."[14]

Pope Benedict XVI made a similar assertion, which was later quoted enthusiastically by his successor Pope Francis, who said that he never tires of repeating it: "Being a Christian is not the result of an ethical choice or a lofty idea, but the encounter with an event, a person, which gives life a new horizon and a decisive direction."[15]

And I will conclude with an ejaculatory prayer which was a favorite of Msgr. Giussani, and which we in Communion and Liberation often pray at the conclusion of communal prayer: *Veni Sancte Spiritus, veni per Mariam.*

"Come Holy Spirit, come through Mary." When the Holy Spirit comes through Mary, what happens? Jesus comes in the flesh. So to pray *Veni Sancte Spiritus, veni per Mariam* is to pray "Come, Lord Jesus." It is to beg that Jesus come in a way that I, who am no angel but a poor sinner who is spirit and flesh, can see with my eyes and touch with my hands and hear with my ears. If I do not recognize and welcome Jesus as he manifests himself in my daily life in the particular ways that he chooses, *I am a resounding gong or clanging cymbal* (1 Cor 13:1). When I am humble enough to be open to his presence, then, as Gabriel assured Mary at the verge of the Incarnation, *nothing will be impossible for God* (Lk 1:37).

Veni Sancte Spiritus, veni per Mariam.

NOTES

❦

1. Bernard of Clairvaux, *Sermo 1 in Epiphania Domini*, 1–2: PL 133, 141–143, quoted in *The Liturgy of the Hours*, Vol. I: Advent Season, Christmas Season (New York: Catholic Book Publishing, 1975), 446. Office of Readings, December 29.

2. Julián Carrón, "The beat of the heart [of God] is pity on your nothingness," in *"I have loved you with an everlasting love. I have had pity on your nothingness,"* Exercises of the Fraternity of Communion and Liberation, tr. Sheila Beatty (Denver: Human Adventure Books, 2016), 33.

3. The Easter Proclamation (Exsultet), The Easter Vigil in the Holy Night, *Roman Missal*, 3rd typical edition, 2011; see CCC 410–412.

4. Luigi Giussani, "Recognizing Christ," in *A Presence with the Gaze*, Exercises of the Fraternity of Communion and Liberation, tr. Patrick Stevenson (Denver: Human Adventure Books, 2015), 67. Msgr. Giussani has many meditations on this Gospel passage which I would recommend for further reflection on the Incarnation.

5. Luigi Giussani, *At the Origin of the Christian Claim* (Montréal: McGill-Queen's University Press, 1998), 31.

6. Augustine, *On the Trinity*, XV.19.37.

7. Luigi Giussani, *Why the Church?* (Montréal: McGill-Queen's University Press, 2001), 131-133.

8. Jean Daniélou, *The Angels and Their Mission According to the Fathers of the Church*, tr. David Heimann (Allen, Tex.: Thomas More Publishing, 1987), 34.

9. John Chrysostom, *Serm asc.*, 4, quoted in Daniélou, 35.

10. John Chrysostom, *Serm asc.*, 3, quoted in Daniélou, 37.

11. Daniélou, 37.

12. Thérèse of the Child Jesus and the Holy Face to Maurice Bellière, July 26, 1897, in Patrick Ahern, *Maurice and Thérèse: Story of a Love* (New York: Doubleday, 1998), 18.

13. Maurice Bellière to Thérèse of the Child Jesus and the Holy Face, August 5, 1897, in Ahern, *Maurice and Thérèse*, 199.

14. John Paul II, Message to Monsignor Luigi Giussani, Founder of the "Communion and Liberation" Movement and Fraternity, February 11, 2002, 2.

15. Benedict XVI, Encyclical Letter *Deus caritas est* (December 25, 2005), 1, quoted in Francis, Apostolic Exhortation *Evangelii Gaudium* (November 24, 2013), 7.